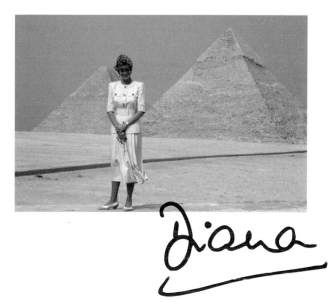

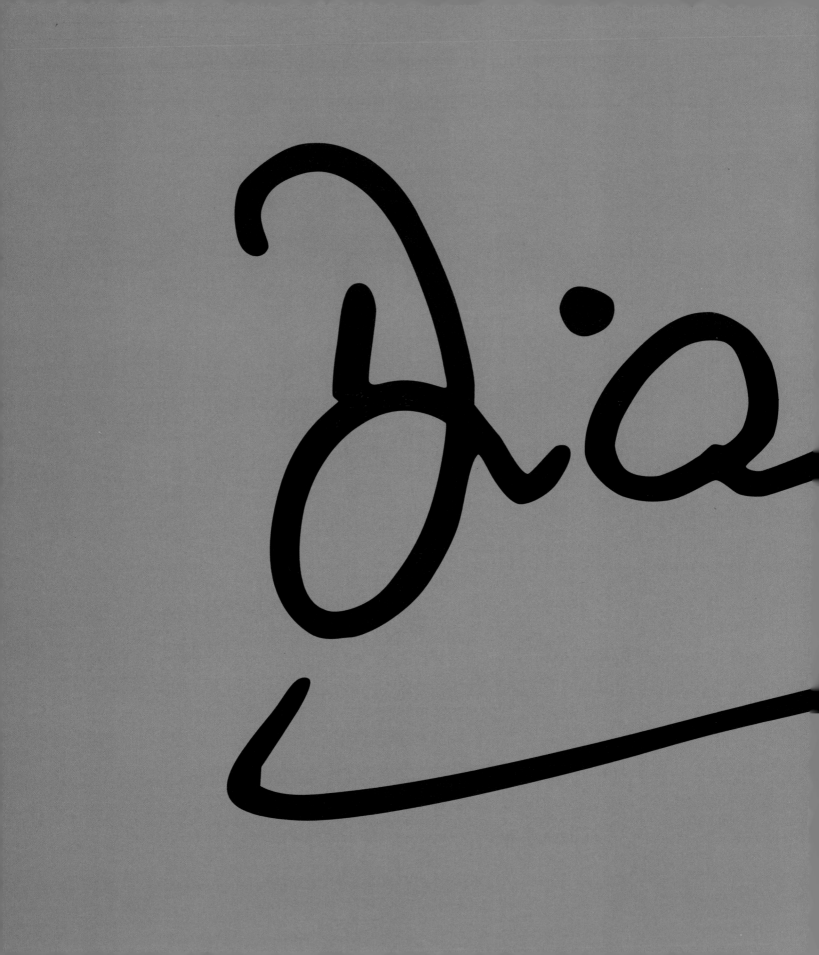

HER LIFE & HER LEGACY

ANTHONY HOLDEN

RANDOM HOUSE

NEW YORK

In memory of Princess Diana, Random House will be donating half of its profits from the sale of this book to the Pediatric AIDS Foundation.

The Pediatric AIDS Foundation is the leading national nonprofit foundation identifying, funding and conducting critical pediatric AIDS research worldwide. The foundation is working to find ways to prevent the transmission of AIDS from an HIV-infected pregnant woman to her newborn; to prolong and improve the lives of children with HIV; to eliminate HIV in infected children; and to promote education, awareness and compassion about this disease.

For more information, please contact:

Pediatric AIDS Foundation
1311 Colorado Avenue
Santa Monica, CA 90404
(310) 395-9051 or for donations (888) 499-HOPE
http://www.PedAIDS.org

Published in Great Britain by Ebury Press, a division of Random House UK, London.

Library of Congress Cataloging-in-Publication data is available

ISBN 0-375-50139-8

Random House website address: http://www.randomhouse.com/

Printed in the United States of America on acid-free paper

24689753

First U.S. Edition

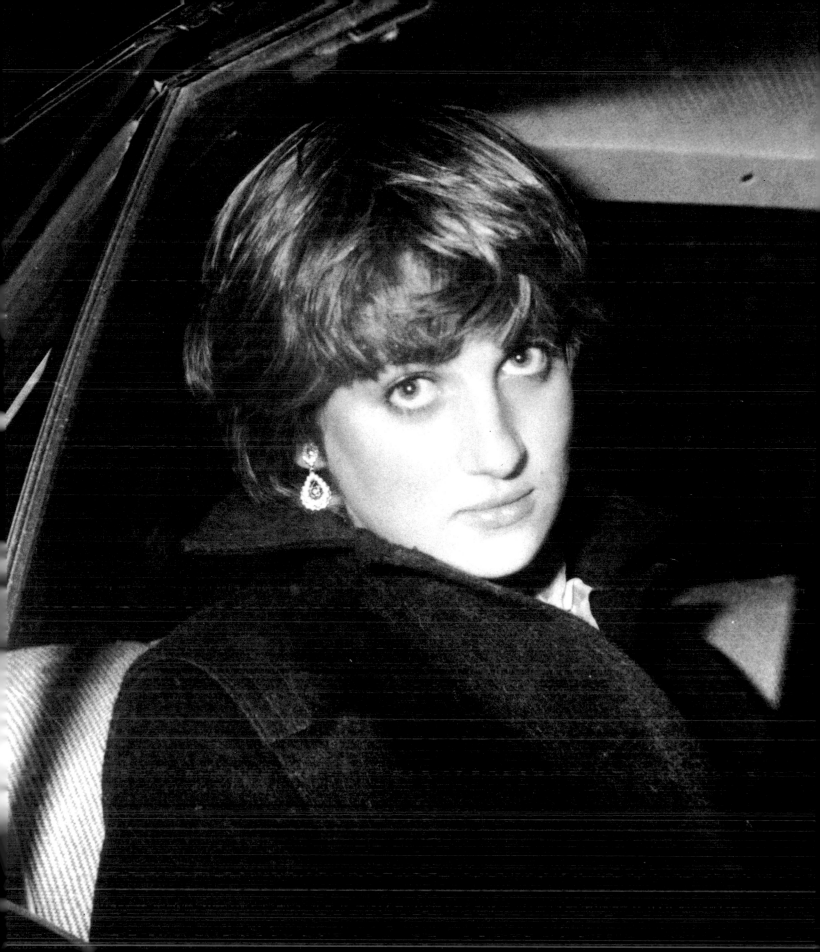

"The people everywhere, not just here in Britain but everywhere, kept faith with Princess Diana. They liked her, they loved her, they regarded her as one of the people. She was the people's princess. That is how she will stay, how she will remain in our hearts for ever."

— TONY BLAIR

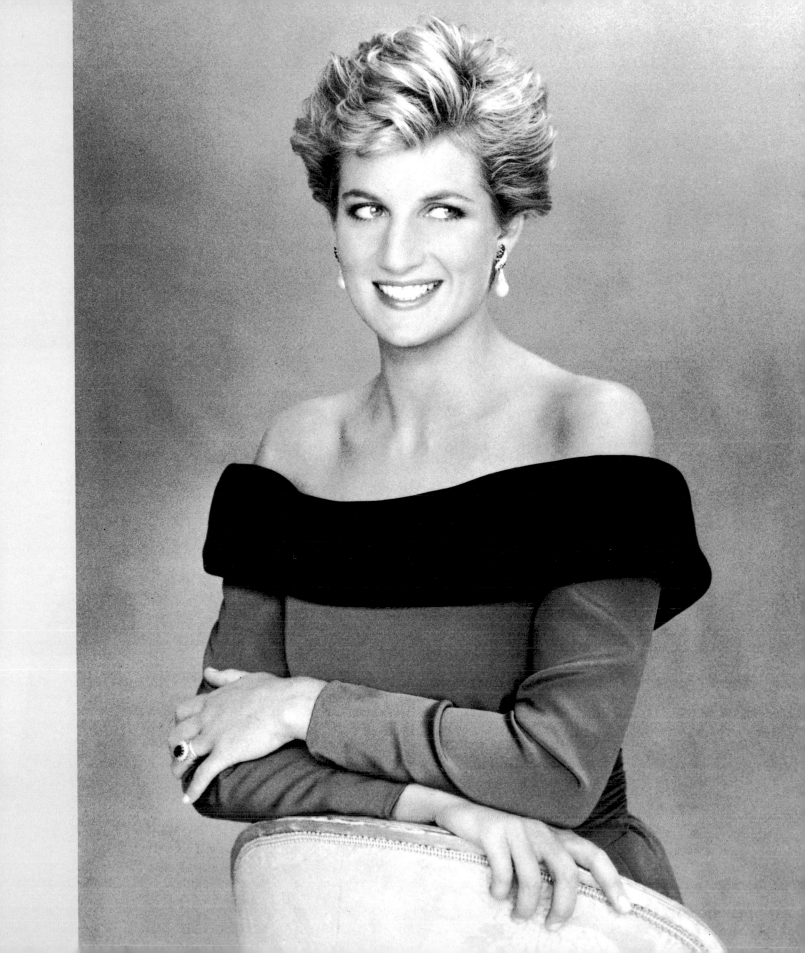

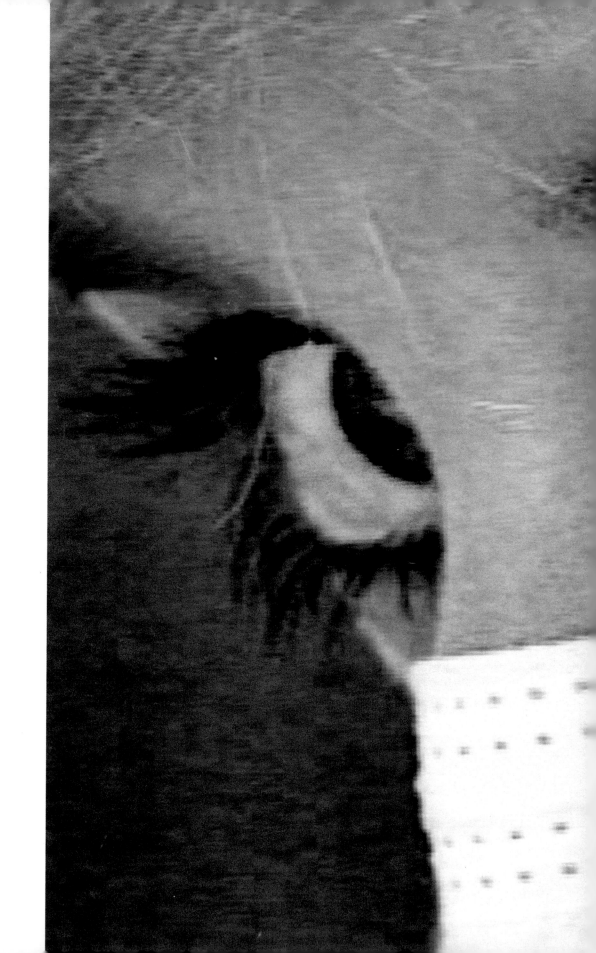

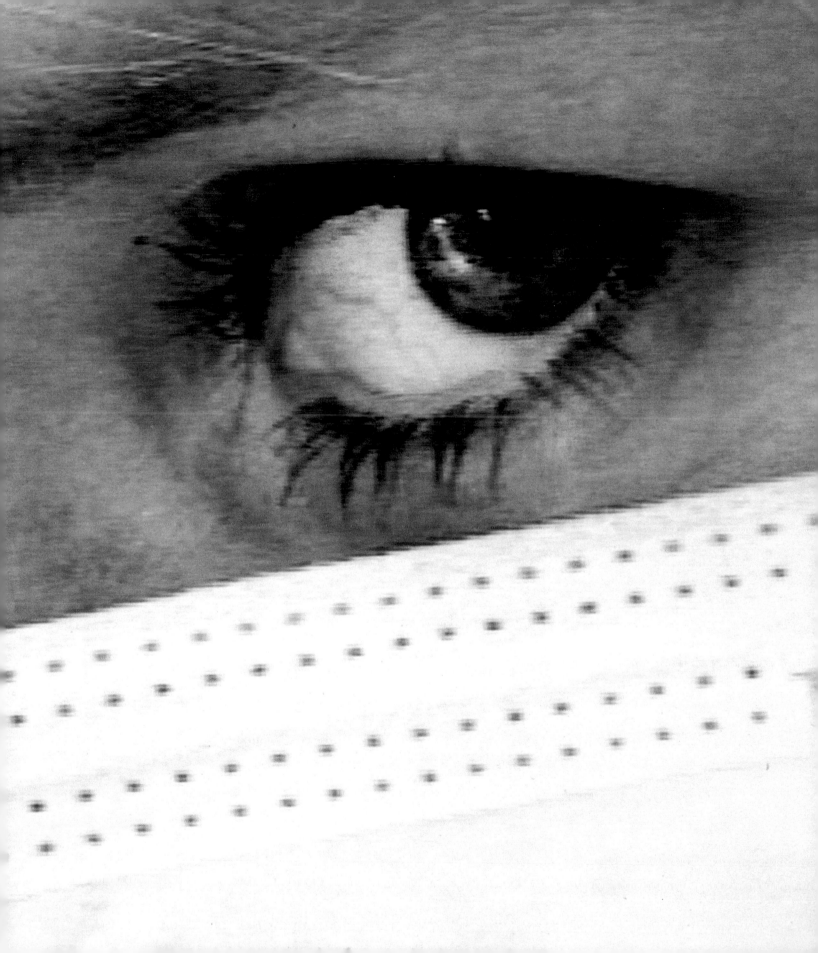

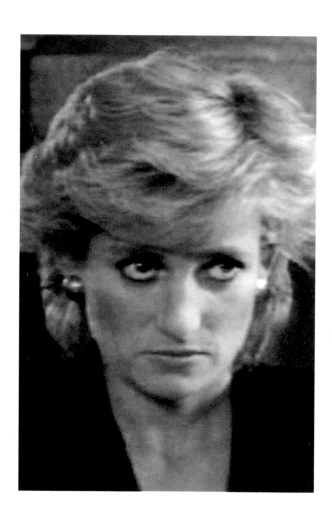

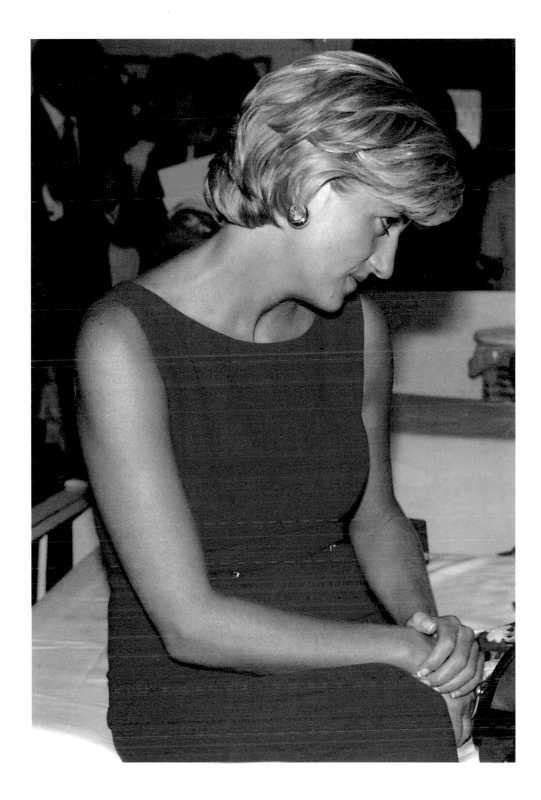

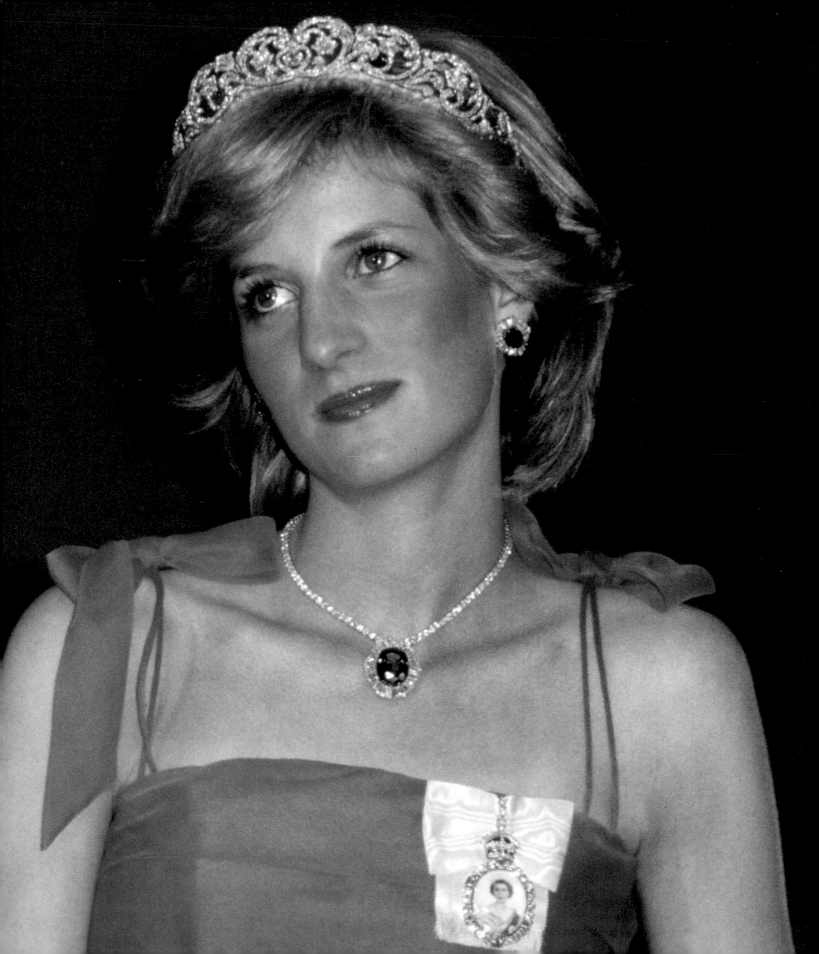

Her troubled, triumphant life and violent, premature death add up to a late twentieth-century parable, an Aesop's fable for the millennium, whose underlying moral only time can tell. But a world moved to a frenzy of grief by her sudden and brutal departure, still in a spasm of post-traumatic shock, already knows that she has changed it for ever, and for the better.

As her fellow-citizens seek tangible ways to honour her memory, to keep her spirit alive among them, their very souls have been touched by the warmth and compassion of Diana, Princess of Wales – a fragile butterfly broken on a media-powered royal wheel, a tenacious tigress in the defence of those, like herself, whom life has victimised, or simply passed by.

In death, as in life, she reached out to thousands more than she ever met, millions more than she ever knew loved her. She still does, and perhaps always will. It is important to remember Diana in the present tense, so potent is the presence she leaves behind in lives touched by no one else in positions remotely approaching authority, while softening the hearts of those who are. For the People's Princess, death removed all irony from the self-imposed sobriquet she privately came to regret, "the Queen of People's Hearts". It was the slogan most frequently used in her people's tributes, and it is how they will remember her. To posterity, her name will resonate as a synonym for sympathy, for learning through her own suffering how to comfort that of others. To those whose lives overlapped with hers, if only from a distance, she remains a blinding reminder of the light which is surely there, however long arriving, at the end of every tunnel.

The way she died, her own light snuffed out in a tunnel whose end she never reached, now seems a bleak metaphor for the darkness through which she was always travelling while shining so bright a light upon others. Like the tragic undercurrents of a life whose surface was all glitter and laughter, glamour and style, the merciless manner of her early death seems now to bear the inevitability of Greek tragedy. Catharsis has yet to come to the rescue of the dazed spectators, but it will. For Diana, Princess of Wales, will live on not just as a person, immortalised by a thousand monuments and idealised in a million memories, but as an idea – an idea whose time, it is clear, was long overdue.

The amazing scenes of mass adulation which followed her death marked a sea-change in recent British history. As an emotionally draining week wore on, with the crowds outside Buckingham Palace dictating what went on inside, Diana seemed to have sparked a bloodless revolution. As centuries of royal protocol were cast aside in response to the public mood, bringing the House of Windsor down from its pedestal to share the grief of its subjects, Diana had signalled an end to the stiff upper lip, to British inhibitions, to centuries of traditionally buttoned-up reserve.

But her death also unleashed deeper feelings overdue an outlet, aching to disprove Margaret Thatcher's dictum that there is "no such thing as society". As they roamed the streets of London in tears, the air pungent with the scent of a million flowers, Britons young enough to have been spared the Blitz had never felt such a sense of community. There was a feeling that the country had

In Australia, 1983.

13

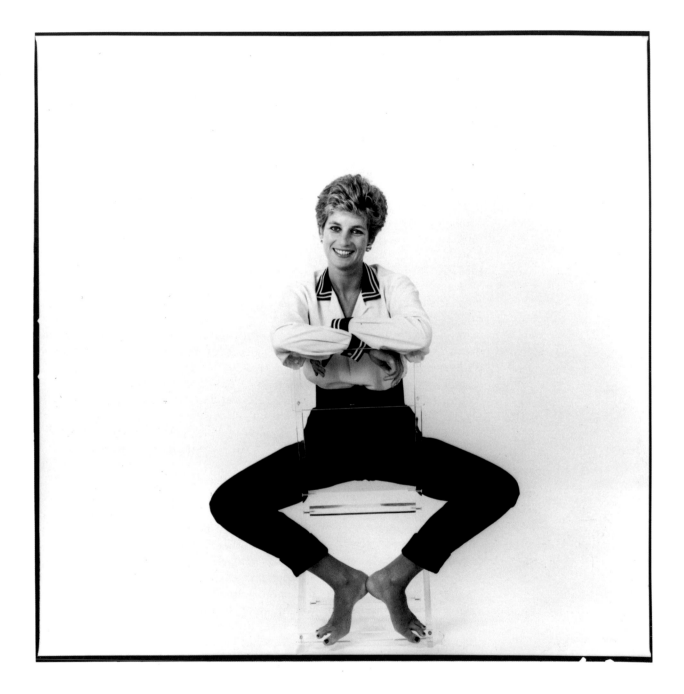

overnight become a warmer, more compassionate, more civilised place.

The brief skirmish between "people power" and "palace power", as the royals seemed slow to share the nation's mourning, was an emphatic rejection of 1980s greed, 1990s mediocrity, and decades – perhaps centuries – of establishment indifference. It was a louder echo of the events of 1 May 1997, only four months earlier, when a young prime minister with all the charisma of a new JFK was elected by a stunning landslide, giving Britain a sense of renewal, of escape from its past, after almost two decades of increasingly tired, heedless, patrician rule.

As he became the man of the moment, mediating between monarchy and people, Tony Blair seemed typecast to pick up Diana's torch and carry it boldly forward towards a new future. There were "lessons to be drawn from her life", conceded the Queen, obliged to respond to events rather than (as the monarchy prefers) anticipating them. Was Britain finally escaping its imperial past, cramped by outmoded tradition, and looking with fresh young eagerness to a modernised, European future? So it seemed, thanks to the cult of Diana, as Blair lent the Queen's remarks a more convincing echo: "Something must come of all this."

Amid the crowds who flocked to pay her homage, queuing in the rain all night to sign books of remembrance, keeping open-ended vigil with prayers and candles, bringing so many flowers that the country soon ran out, were many who would never normally attend royal occasions – refugees from the disenfranchised minorities on the margins of modern British life. People disillusioned by politicians and royalty alike had looked to Diana, it became clear, as their only true champion in what seemed an alien world. If she was to some extent an anti-establishment figure, carving out a niche for herself as a royal rebel, even a royal pariah, she can never have known the depth of the chord she struck with all manner of social outcasts, their kinship born of parallel feelings of rejection. As grief-stricken as the most devout of monarchists, they had lost their patron saint, a Boadicea of the oppressed. Deprived of her famous hugs, both literal and metaphorical, they sobbed and hugged each other.

In that extraordinary week between her death and her funeral, perfect strangers comforted each other in the middle of London's streets, after the sheer weight of mourners had unilaterally banished traffic elsewhere. Britons were openly touching each other, patting each other on the shoulder, holding hands, embracing. It was another of Diana's remarkable legacies, implanted in the national consciousness by ubiquitous images of her stroking and hugging sick children, taking them in her arms and cradling their heads on her breast. Tactile values, the importance of touch, were becoming a central part of her posthumous iconography. As her friend Rosa Monckton put it, "Diana told me about the importance of touch: of how just cupping her hands round someone's face gave huge comfort, and transcended all barriers of race and language." This was the universal language of "a very British girl", in her brother Charles's words, "who transcended nationality".

In countries far beyond her native shores, Diana's name will survive as a

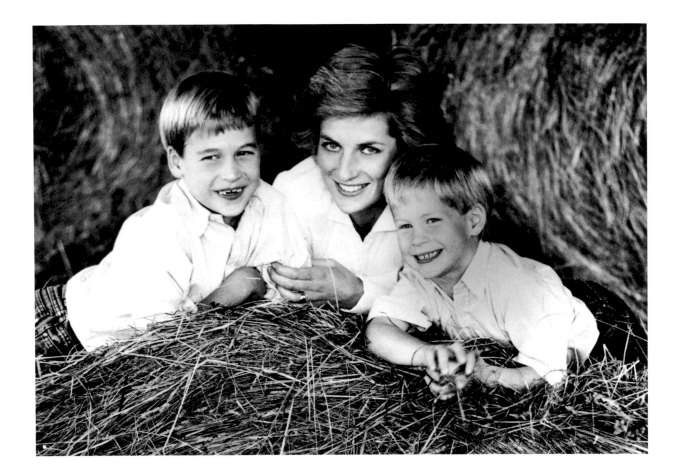

"I admired and respected her – for her energy and commitment to others, and especially for her devotion to her two boys."
– H.M. QUEEN ELIZABETH II

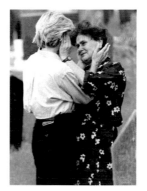

Above, Sarajevo, August 1997.

Left, mother and sons at Highgrove, 1990.

reminder that the world can be a kinder place than it often seems, in an age driven less by spiritual than material values. "Anywhere I see suffering," she said, "is where I want to be, doing what I can.... Nothing gives me greater pleasure than to help the most vulnerable people in society." That she was herself so visibly vulnerable, of course, only deepened her appeal. "All over the world," as Charles Spencer put it, "she was a symbol of selfless humanity, all over the world a standard-bearer for the rights of the downtrodden." On top of her high-profile work for global charities and causes, her death prompted thousands of tales of unpublicised private kindnesses – letters to sick children, phone calls to their parents – emphatically giving the lie to those who had said it was all public relations. In life, she had even had a defiant slogan with which to answer them: "You cannot comfort the afflicted without afflicting the comfortable."

Whatever her own faults, and she was always the first to admit them, Diana looked for the best in others, and found it in places which surprised even them. Those indifferent to her in life were moved by her death to a degree which crept up and ambushed them. They felt impelled to re-examine their own values, and their prejudices, quite as much as those who had always been with her from a distance, supporting her through the many public and private trials by which she always seemed to be dogged. Diana's Army, who massed in such bewildering numbers to mourn her, reluctant to let her go, suffer still from a sense of loss which passes their comprehension, and may never entirely heal.

The greatest loss, of course, is that felt by her two bereft sons. Diana's primary role in life, whomever else she sought to comfort, was that of a devoted, ever-present mother. "They mean everything to me," she said of William and Harry. "I always feed my children love and affection. It's so important."

Despite those poor boys' prior claim, families all over Britain and America, the countries of the Commonwealth and the remotest corners of the world still grieve as if they had lost one of their own. Regarding Diana as one of themselves, these distant relatives could only look on in dismay as the family which had made her famous, but rejected her in life, sought to reclaim her in death from the "blood family" whence she came. Even in death Diana was causing trouble. It was everyday trouble, of a kind familiar to all those surrogate families around the world, so familiar as to raise some knowing smiles amid the gloom. It was trouble she was powerless to control. But, as always with Diana, it was trouble from which something positive would emerge, at whatever cost to her.

Trouble, in a cloistered, castellated royal world slow to adjust to the modern age, was all too often the price of Diana's compassion. Easily satirised in a cynical age, as it continually was in her lifetime, the ability to lend comfort to others is a rare and precious gift which became her mission in life. It is forged, she went to her grave believing, through having "been there" oneself, knowing what it is like to reach out in the darkness and find no one there.

Five years before her death, in Rome in 1992, Diana nodded with evident feeling when Mother Teresa of Calcutta told her publicly: "To heal other people you have to suffer yourself." Despite an age-gap of half a century, they were

DIANA

With Mother Teresa in New York,
June 1997.

friends who would die within days of each other, soul sisters of compassion with parallel global force fields. Where Diana was perhaps more martyr than saint, Teresa may have been more saint than martyr. While the world attempted an unofficial canonisation of Diana within hours of her death, the Vatican was offering Mother Teresa a "fast-track" to sainthood within days of hers.

As grief-wracked emotions spun out of control, it was all too easy to lose sight of the insight the older woman had offered the younger, a truth towards which she was already feeling her own way. To reach the point where she was able to dispense her unique, self-taught brand of compassion, Diana had been obliged to endure her own fair share of suffering. It began almost as soon as she was aware she was alive.

In life, as she would be the first to giggle, Diana was no saint. So in death, as her brother said with such passion, she would not wish to be made a martyr. Remember her rather as a force of nature, whose spontaneity and natural charm, defiant of tradition, precedent and authority, was evident from the very first, in the face of relentless negativity. Even her birth – emblematically, it now seems – failed to please everyone. She was supposed to have been a boy.

"She was a very great friend in love with the poor."
— MOTHER TERESA

EARLY YEARS

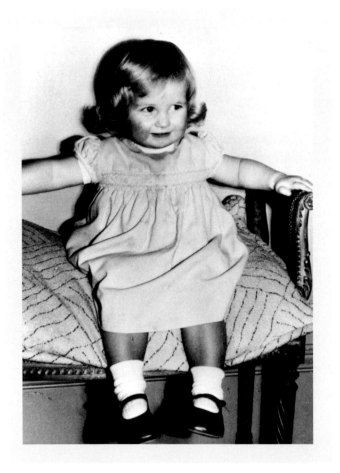

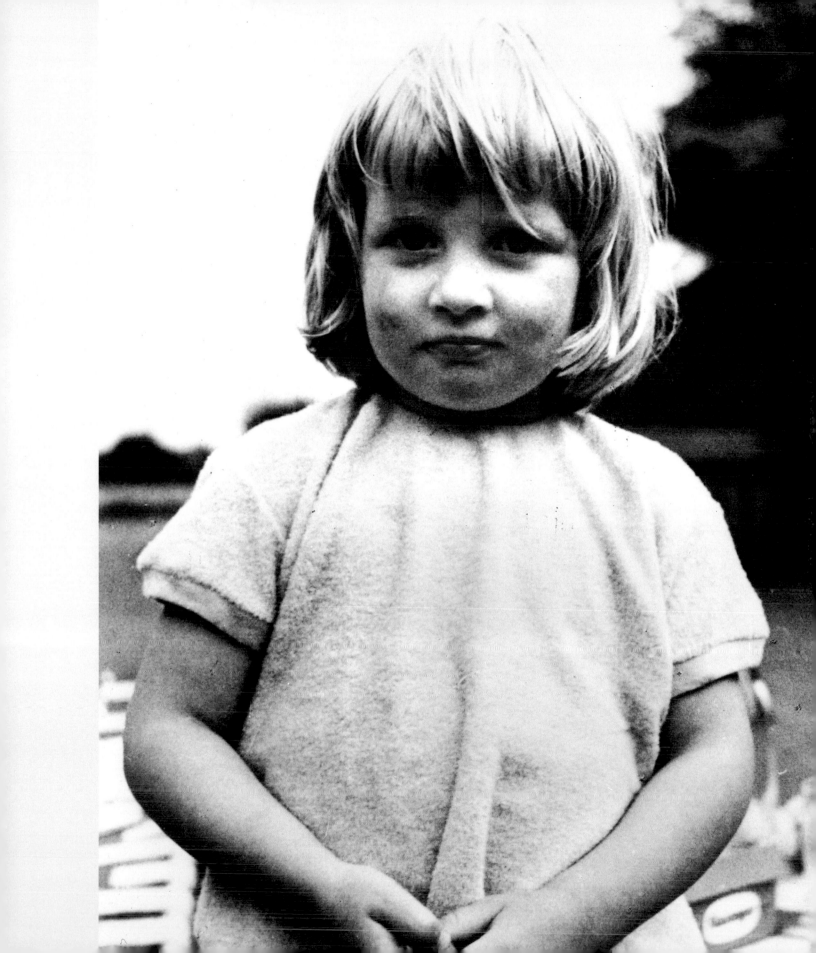

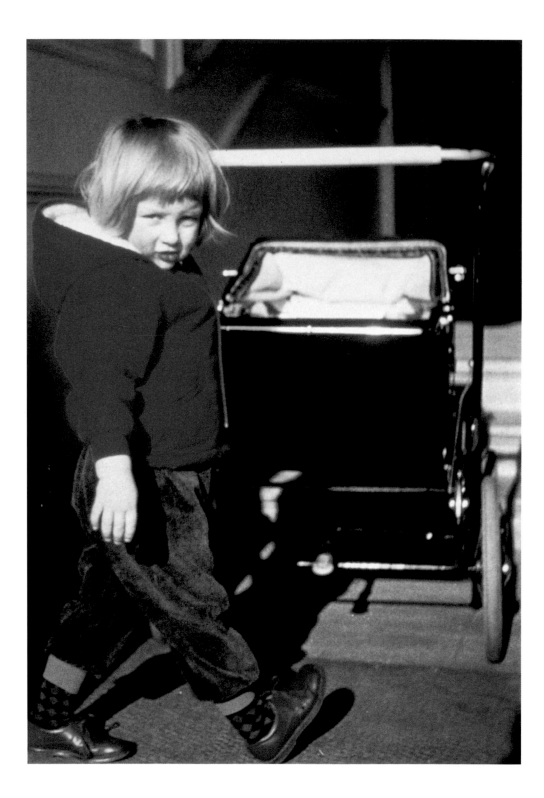

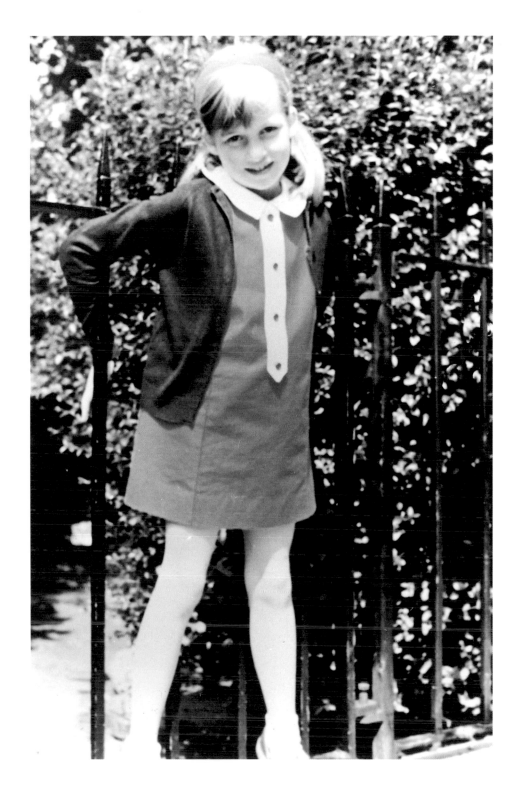

Right, aged 7.
Left, aged 2.

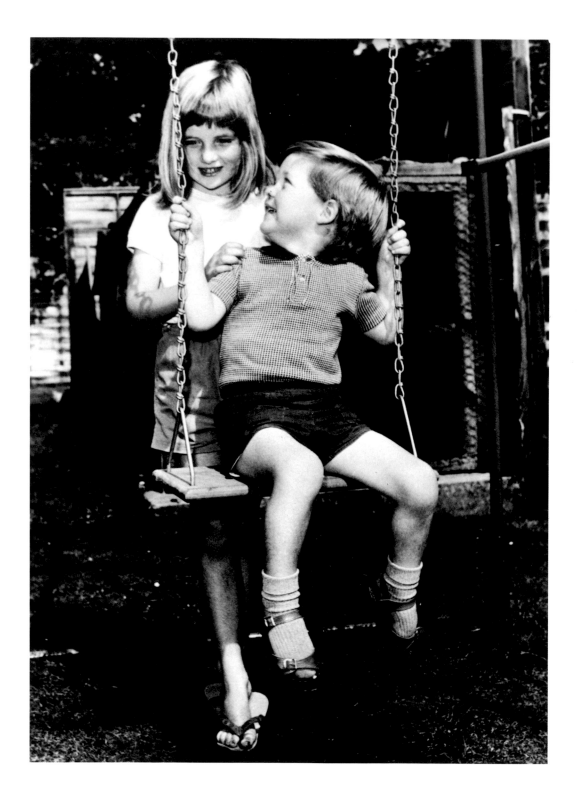

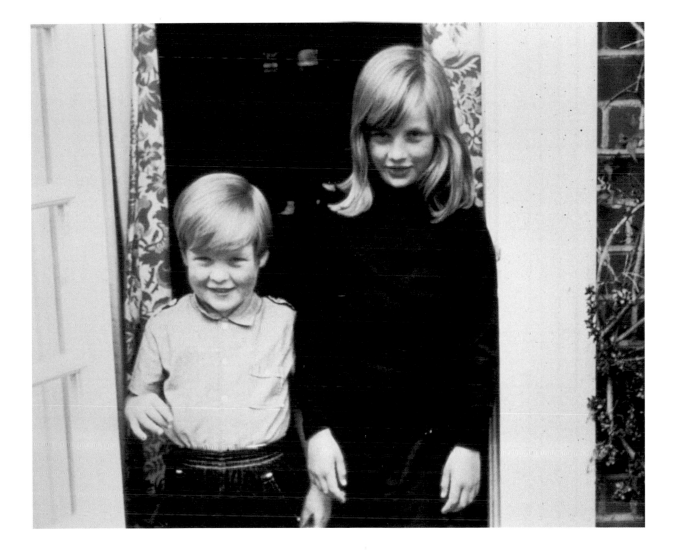

With Charles, Viscount
Althorp, *left*, at Park
House, Sandringham,
aged 5; and (*above*) in
Berkshire, aged 6.

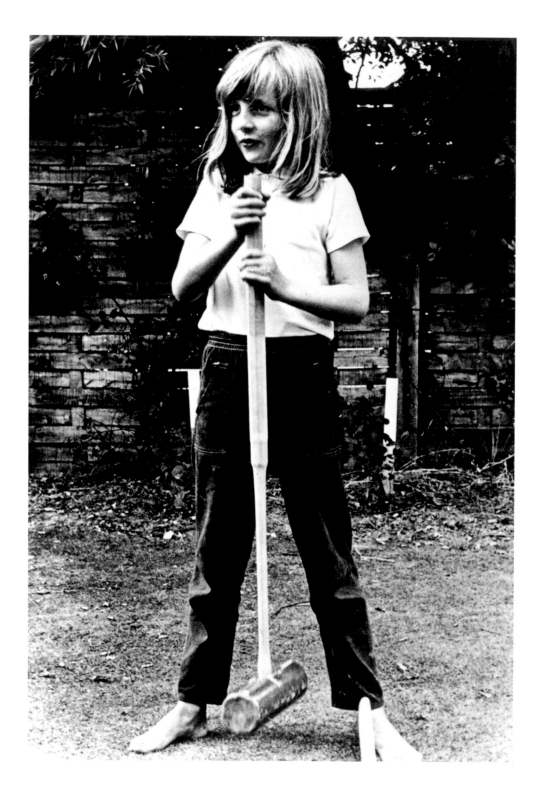

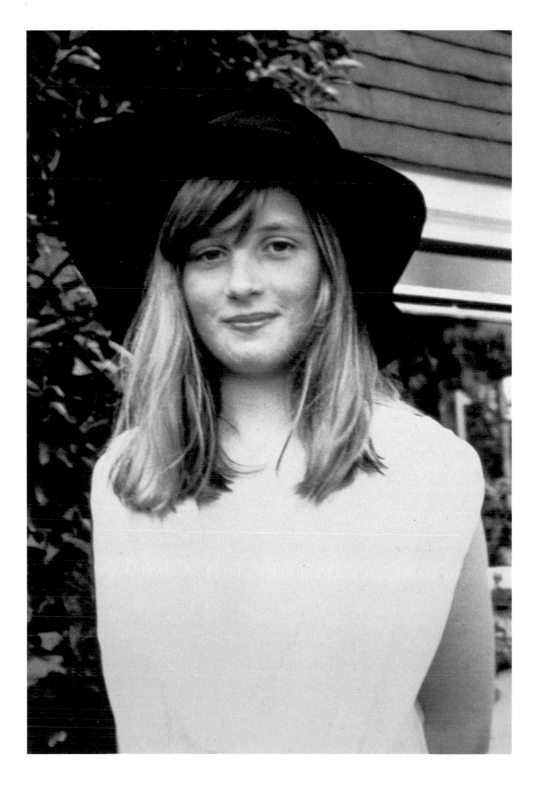

Opposite, at Itchenor, West Sussex, aged 9; and, *right*, a few years later.

Overleaf, at Oban, Scotland, aged 13.

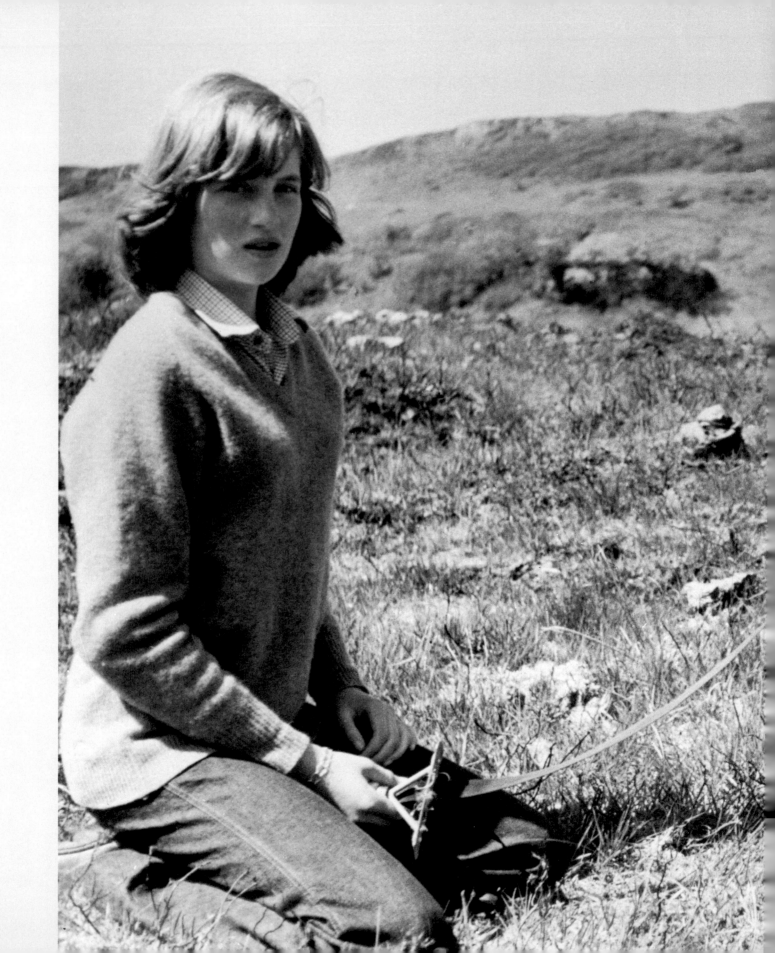

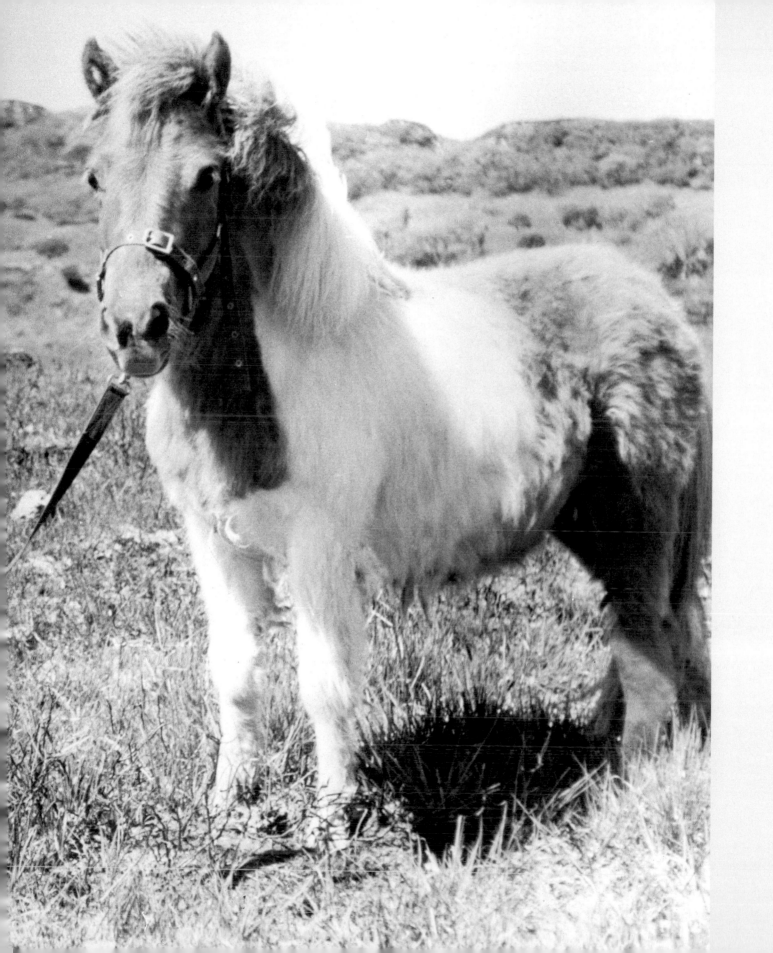

Towards the end of the Middle Ages, when wool was so important to England that the Lord Chancellor presided over the House of Lords while sitting (as he still does) on the Woolsack, the Spencers were among a handful of old English families to make a huge fortune simply by owning sheep. In 1506, under the Tudors, they acquired the estate of Althorp in Northamptonshire, where they built the handsome home which is to this day their family seat. A century later Sir Robert Spencer was reputed to be the richest man, in terms of ready cash, in the kingdom. In 1603 he was made Baron Spencer, one of the first peers of England created by the new Stuart king, James I. The line of descent has remained unbroken ever since.

Lady Diana Frances Spencer, in other words, was born more English than the royal family, and arguably more royal. But to her future husband and his parents she began life, quite literally, as the girl next door. She was born on 1 July 1961, at Park House, a former hunting lodge on the royal estate at Sandringham, Norfolk, which her father was then renting from the Queen. Edward John, Viscount Althorp, heir to the 7th Earl Spencer, and his wife, Frances, (née Roche), younger daughter of the 4th Baron Fermoy, were familiar figures at court. Diana's father had been the Queen's equerry on her coronation tour of Australia in 1954, and her grandmother was one of the Queen Mother's few lifelong intimates.

After losing one son in infancy, the couple already had two daughters, Sarah and Jane. At the fourth attempt, Viscount "Johnny" Althorp had gone to the lengths of lighting bonfires to greet a male heir to the historic title in his charge. Amid the natural joy of childbirth, however, a note of dismay greeted the arrival of another girl. The pressure on her mother to produce a male heir was a pressure Diana herself would one day know; already it was causing irreparable damage to her parents' marriage – the same hurtful, creeping corrosion she too would one day endure, though for very different reasons. Diana herself was to outdo her mother by effortlessly breeding male heirs, to a far grander title, with all the natural magic she seemed to bring to every task she undertook. It was a gratifying corrective to the way she herself came into the world.

The man she was eventually to marry, heir to the loftiest hereditary title on earth, was one of the first to lay eyes on the little blonde bundle who would play so fateful a role in his own life. Charles, Prince of Wales, even at twelve the magnanimous landlord, swiftly dropped by the Althorps' home with a celebratory bottle of champagne. Perhaps, with his own heritage in mind, he also offered a word of sympathy to the frustrated Earl-in-waiting, who was soon to order gynaecological tests on a wife who did not seem capable of breeding him male heirs. It would be three more years before the Althorps at last had a son to ensure the Spencer succession. Proudly they won royal permission to name him Charles, after their illustrious young neighbour.

By then, however, Diana's own young life was already going into eclipse, the brief sunshine of her early years obscured by clouds which would never entirely clear. The defining moment of her childhood came when she was just six years old. Frances Spencer's youngest daughter sat forlornly alone, on the cold stone floor of the house where she had been born, the only home she had ever known, as domestic staff bustled around loading her mother's worldly goods into a waiting car. There was a scrunch of feet on the gravel, the slam of a car door, the sound of an engine starting, then slowly receding into the distance as the whole house fell ominously silent. Diana's mother was gone, never to return.

The Spencer marriage had started, as it was to end, in a blaze of publicity. In 1954 Frances had been the youngest bride this century to have married in Westminster Abbey, with the young new Queen and her husband, Philip, among the guests. By the birth of her son ten years later, she had grown so weary of life with Johnny Spencer, whom she subsequently sued on the grounds of cruelty, that she was prepared to surrender not merely her title, but her children, to escape him. "Suddenly," as one of the servants put it, "she just wasn't there any more."

It was that scrunching sound on the gravel, Diana used to say, which she could still hear thirty years later. It haunted her every subsequent day, and kept her awake at night. As soon as they were old enough to understand anything, the four Spencer children – Sarah, Jane, Diana and Charles – knew that their parents' marriage was not the field of dreams they had fondly imagined. They grew up to a descant of raised voices, which may have ended at home that dark day in 1967, but continued through the law courts for two more years in one of the bitterest high-society divorce cases of the day. Johnny Spencer countersued his wife on the grounds of her adultery with a wallpaper heir named Peter Shand-Kydd, into whose arms she had fled. Feelings in the family ran so high that Frances' own mother, the Queen Mother's friend Ruth, Lady Fermoy, testified against her.

Her parents' divorce case was about as painful for Diana as these things can possibly be. Like the rest of the nation, the eight-year-old girl could only watch via the national newspapers as her father mobilised sufficient character witnesses from the British aristocracy to render her mother's cruelty suit hopeless. Custody of the children – most unusually, then as now – was granted to her father.

As Diana was transplanted to a country boarding school, her mother removed herself to the remote north-west of Scotland, where she settled into a happier new domesticity as Mrs Shand-Kydd. Henceforth, as her brother Charles recalled, Diana and her siblings would spend their school holidays shuttling the 450 miles between Norfolk and Oban. Subsequent relations with her mother, however affectionate, would always be shot through with tension. It was much the same with her father. Diana loved both her parents as much as any dutiful child; but their love for her and her siblings, in their different ways, was scarcely unconditional. Scars were already being etched on Diana's young psyche.

She was fourteen when, in 1975, her father became the 8th Earl Spencer on the death of his own father, Jack, and moved his family into the ancestral Spencer seat at Althorp (pronounced "Al-trup"). A 450-year-old, 1,500-acre stately home boasting a fine collection of old masters, it also conferred on the new Earl the less welcome legacy of crippling death duties. Less than a year later, in the midst of dire financial difficulties, he remarried – another divorcée, and a somewhat exotic one in the shape of Raine, Countess Dartmouth, much loved by British gossip columnists as an outspoken London politician and the daughter of the prolific, romance novelist Barbara Cartland.

Raine Dartmouth's arrival as their stepmother caused dismay among the growing Spencer children. Her flamboyant style grated on them, and the sleepy halls of Althorp were not accustomed to her brand of new-broom dynamism. Raine was soon applying her celebrated energies to sprucing the place up, and generating new sources of income. Though some rejuvenation was long overdue, her brisk personal style offended both family and local sensibilities, as she dismissed some long-standing members of staff, opened the house to the paying public, and herself ran a gift shop in the stable block. But the children were soon reassured by the care and affection she lavished on their father, and were finally won over by the devotion with which she nursed him back to health after a near-fatal stroke in 1978, just a week after celebrating Althorp's return to solvency.

By now transplanted to another boarding school in Kent, Diana was regarded as a "thoroughly average" pupil, "a perfectly ordinary little girl who was always kind and cheerful". Though she still saw the younger royals during vacations, she was beginning to make lasting friendships of her own, including with the two girls who would enjoy fleeting fame as her Chelsea flatmates. There was a little gentle teasing as she exchanged letters with the Queen's second son, Prince Andrew, of whom she hung a photograph over her bed. Andrew was just a year older than Diana. One day, giggled her friends, there might even be a romance.

The rumours pursued her when she left school at sixteen, without one O level to her name, to travel the well-worn path of well-born girls to finishing school in Switzerland. She lasted only six weeks, fleeing abruptly, pleading homesickness. All she brought back with her from Montreux was a smattering of French and some early experience on the nursery ski slopes.

Now her father set her up in a flat in London, where she was determined to find a job and build an independent life of her own. But it was during these few months of nervous transition, on the threshold of adulthood, that Diana found herself standing in a ploughed field on a stretch of the Althorp estate known as Nobottle Wood, handing round drinks to members of a visiting shooting party. Among the guests was 30-year-old Charles, Prince of Wales, then squiring her sister Sarah. She found him, Diana subsequently confessed, "pretty amazing". The future king, for his part, noticed for the first time how Sarah's baby sister had blossomed into "a very amusing, and jolly, and attractive" 17-year-old.

Only once, since visiting the youngest Spencer daughter in her cradle, had Charles made any significant gesture towards her. In the summer of 1969, after his investiture at Caernarvon on what happened to be Diana's eighth birthday, the prince had relaxed at Balmoral by writing a children's story for his younger brothers Andrew and Edward, then aged nine and five. Entitled *The Old Man of Lochnagar*, it was eventually to be published, in 1980, with drawings by his friend Sir Hugh Casson. At the time, on returning to Sandringham, Charles ran off an extra copy for the little girl next door who sometimes played with his brothers.

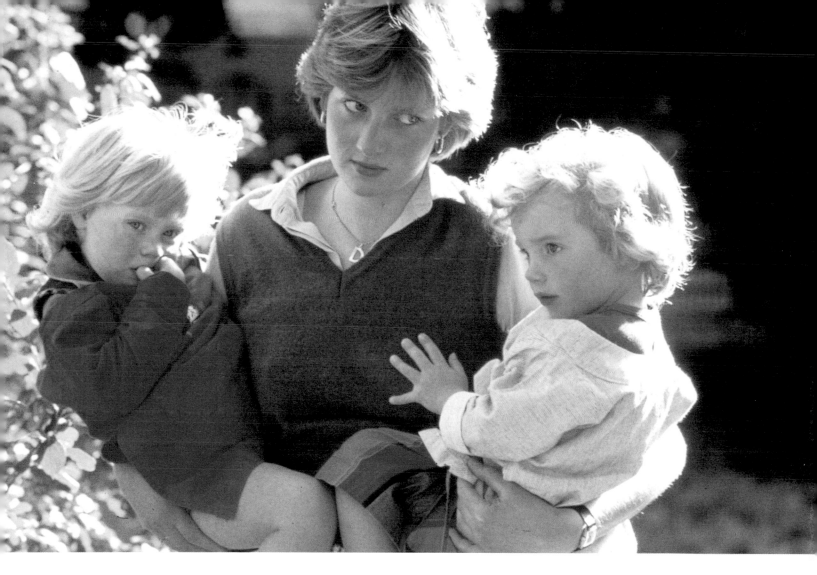

At the Young England nursery school in London, 1980.

"No one who knew Diana will ever forget her. Millions of others who never met her, but felt they knew her, will remember her."
— H.M. QUEEN ELIZABETH II

MARRIAGE

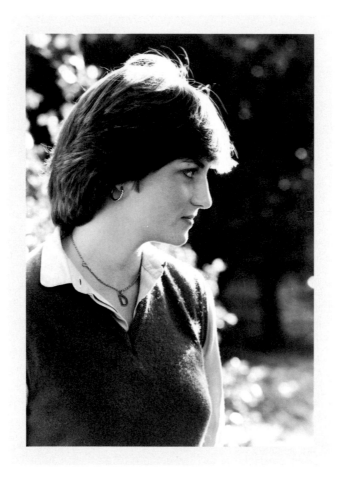

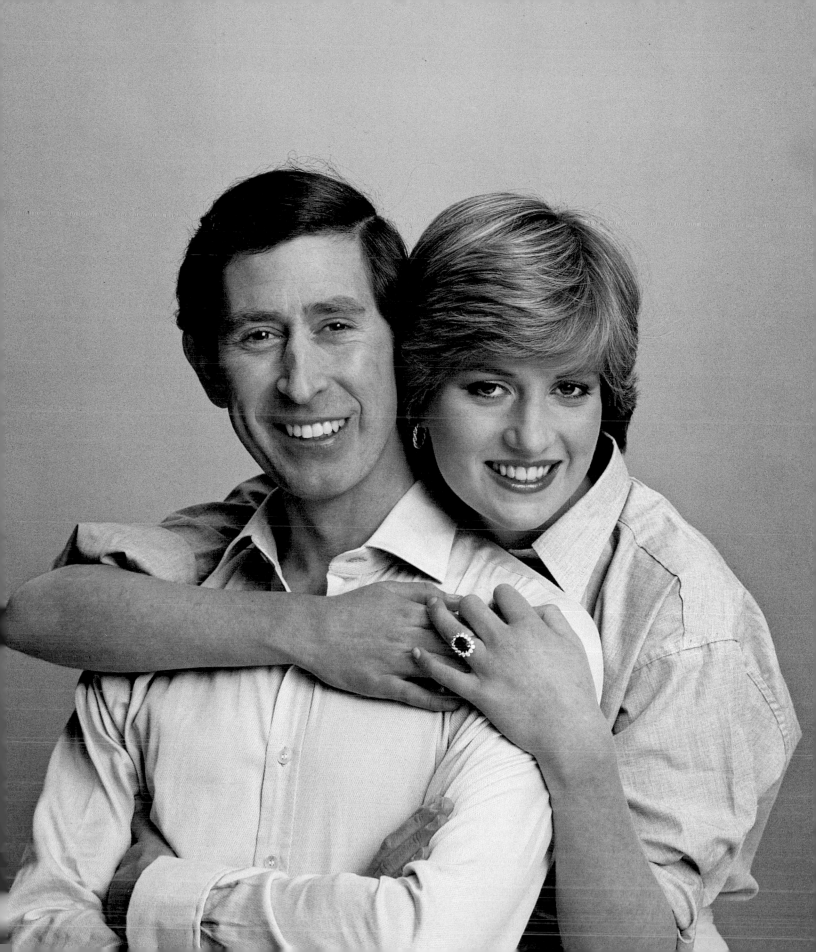

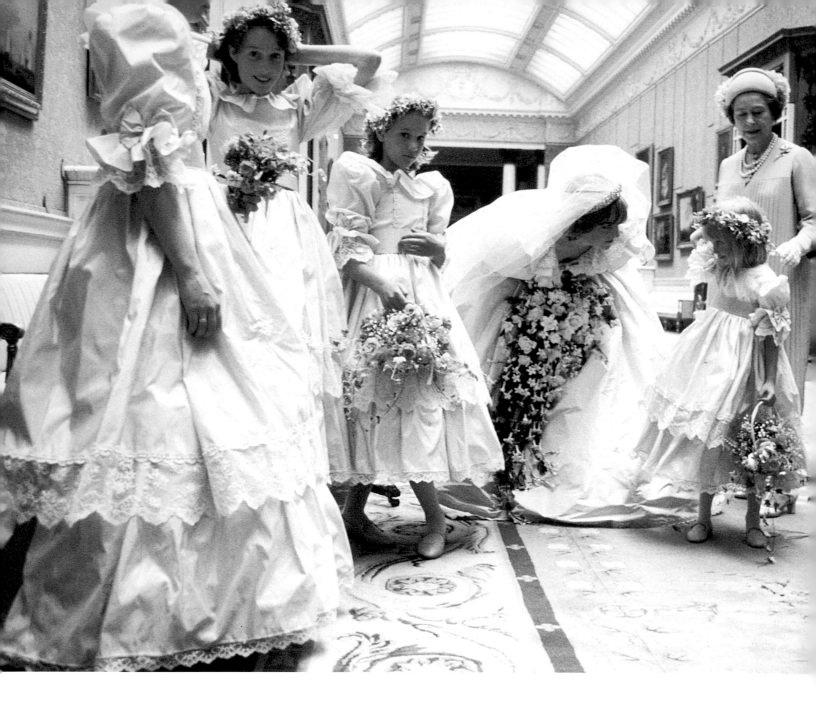

Inside Buckingham Palace, preparing for the wedding, 1981.

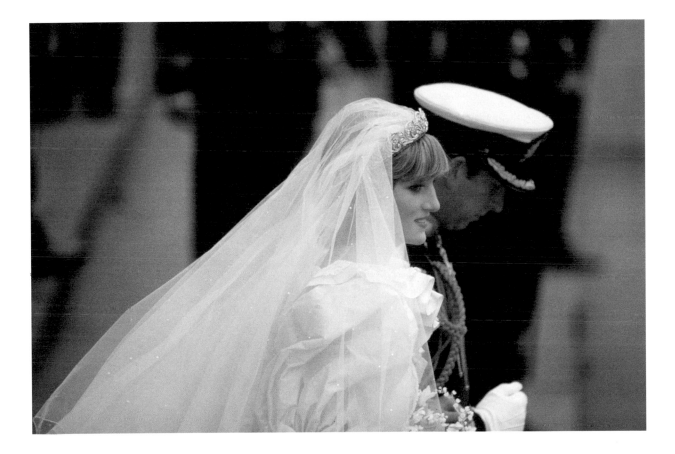

"Charles did love me when we
got married.... If anyone ever
saw the love letters we wrote
to each other, they would
believe that."

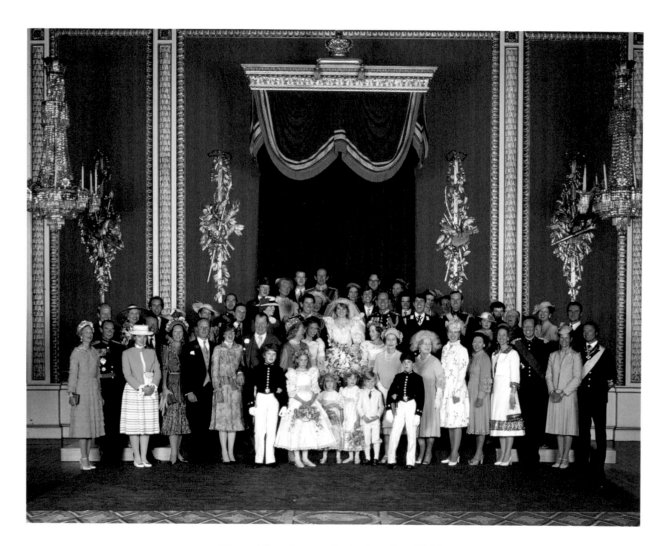

The wedding photographs, by Patrick Lichfield.

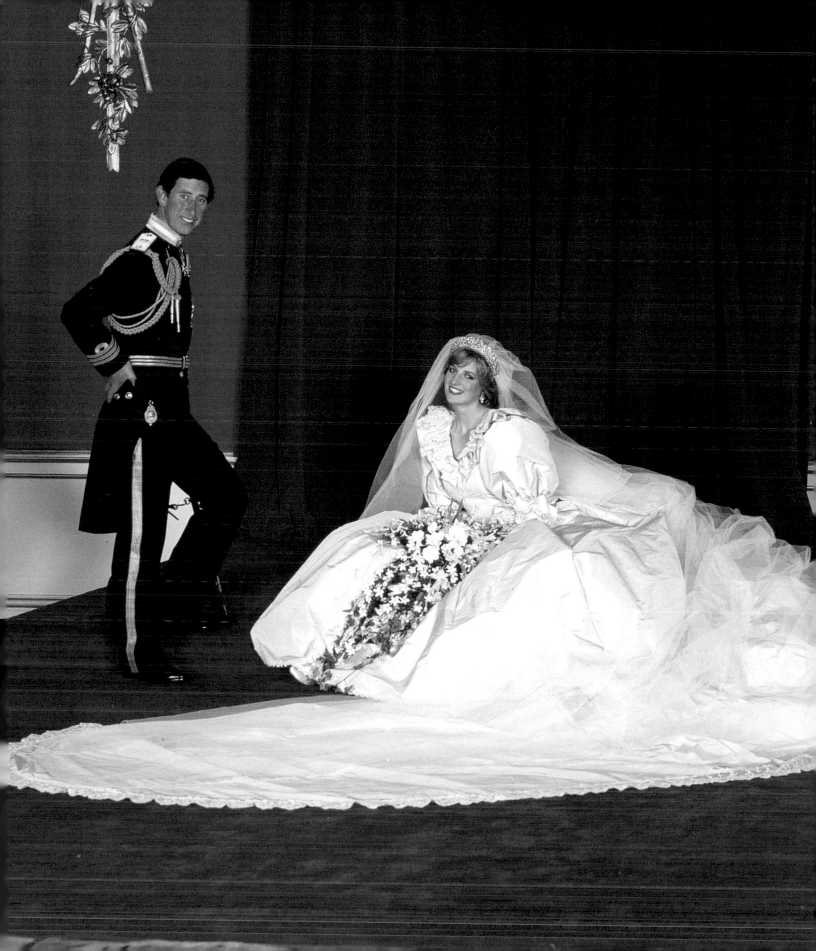

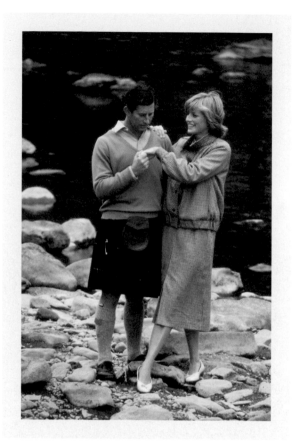

On honeymoon at Balmoral, 1981.

Charles found himself touched by young Diana's tender offers of comfort. "You poor thing," she said to him, "you looked so miserable at Lord Mountbatten's funeral. You need someone to look after you."

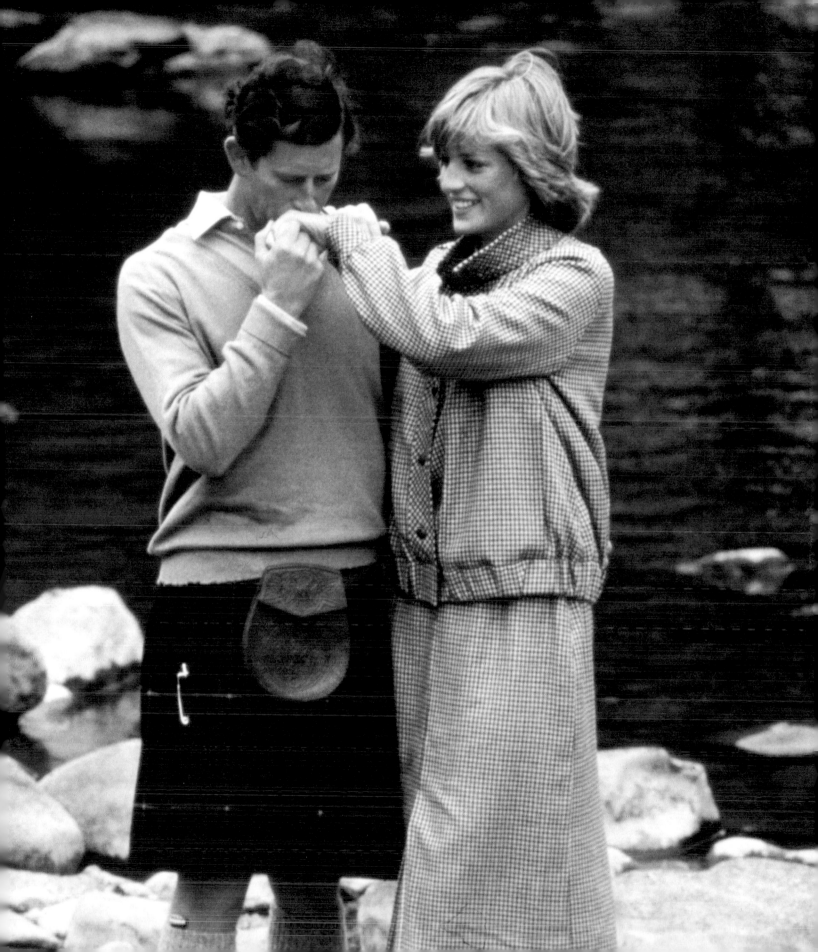

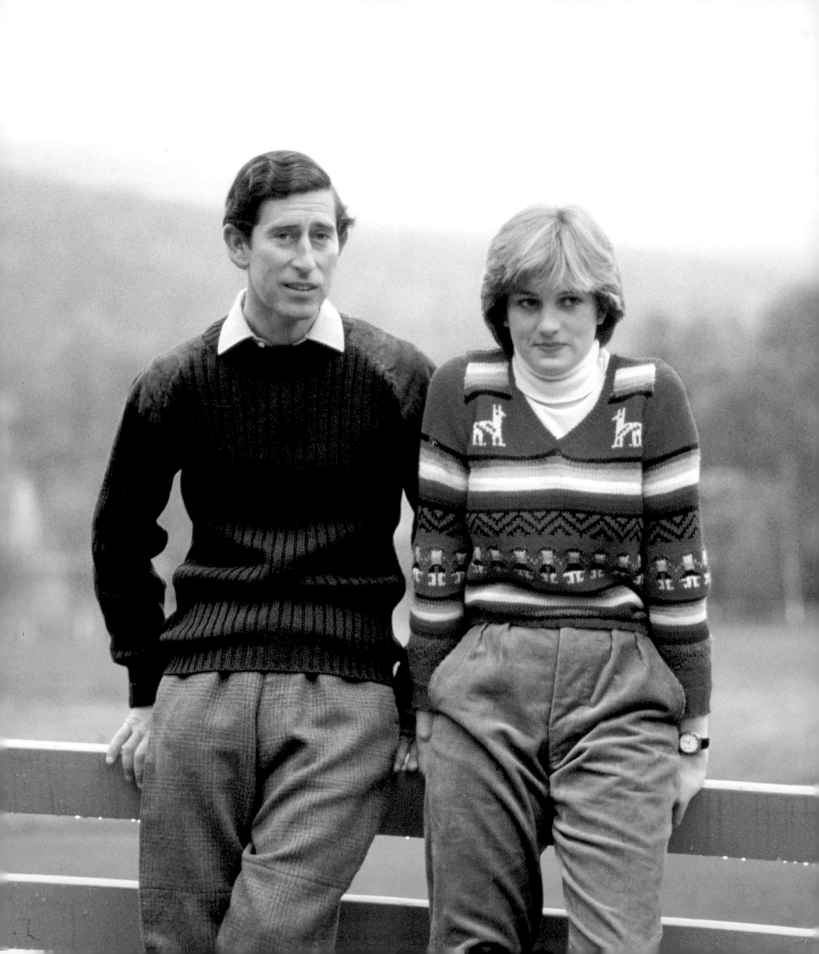

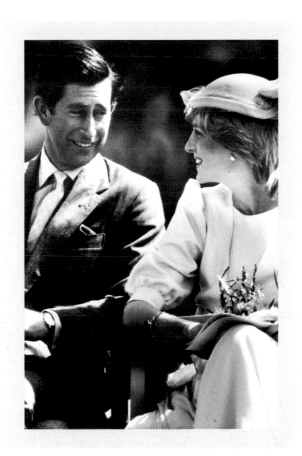

Left, Balmoral, 1981.
Above, Newcastle, 1983.

"Like any marriage, especially when you've had divorced parents like myself, you want to try even harder to make it work. I desperately wanted it to work."

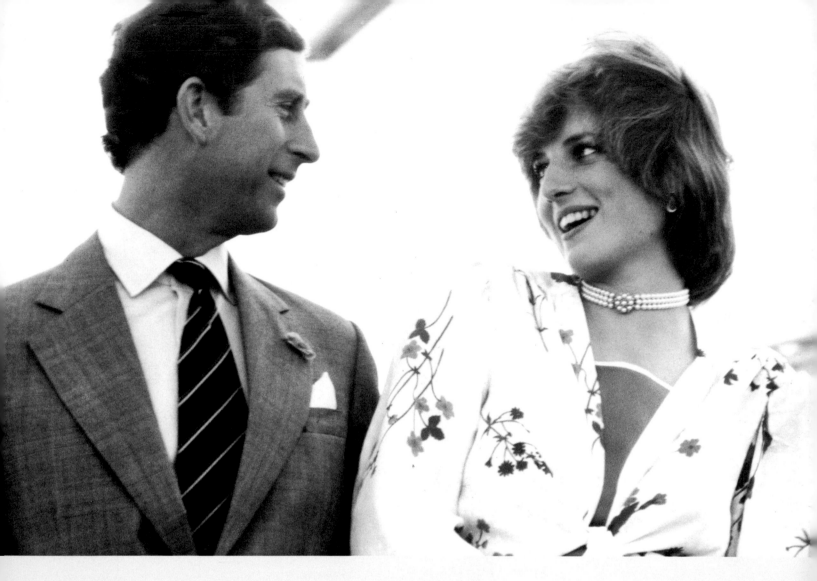

On honeymoon, 1981.

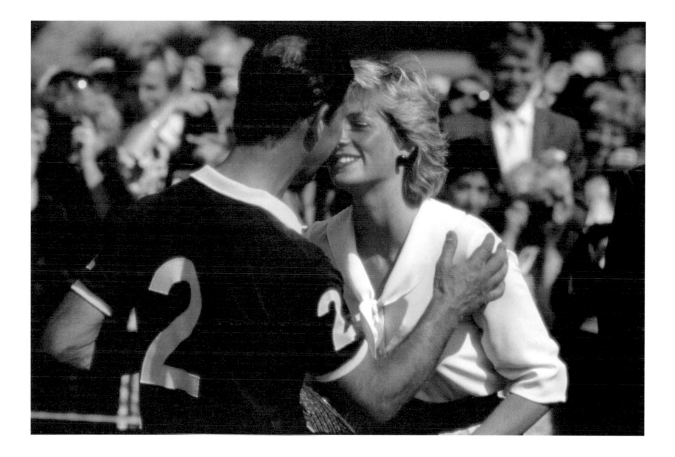

Above and *below left*, Polo at Windsor, summer 1987.
Below right, November 1992.

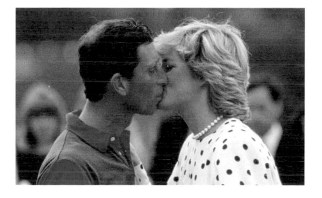
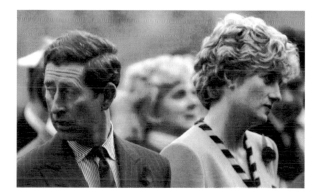

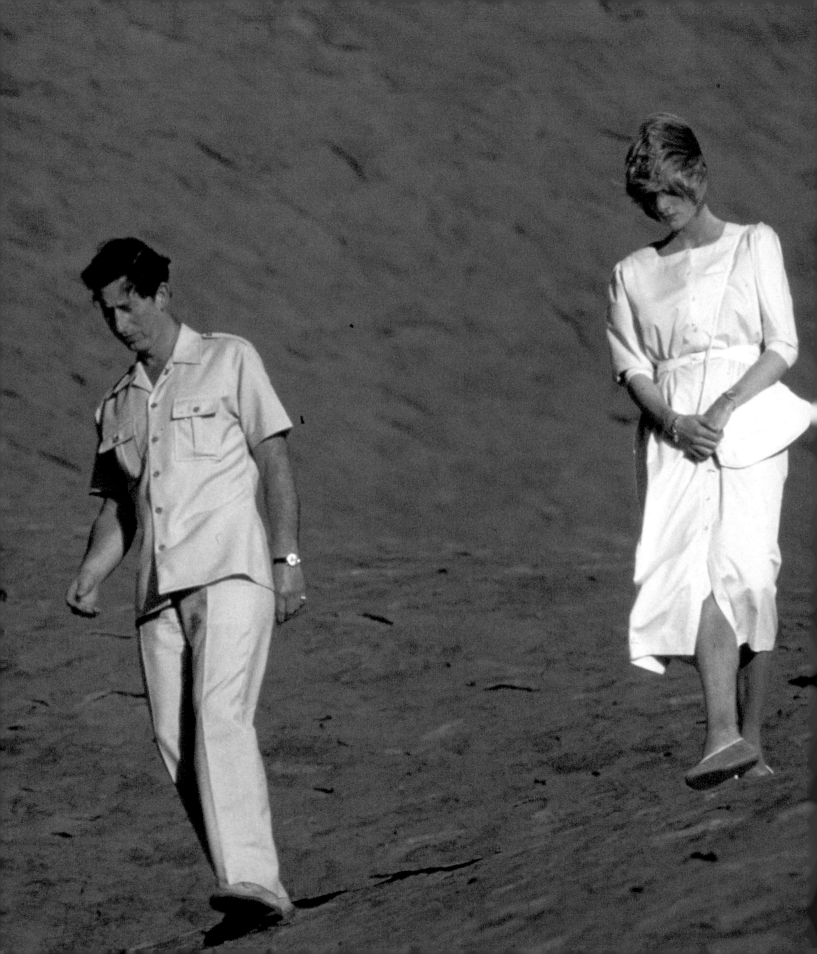

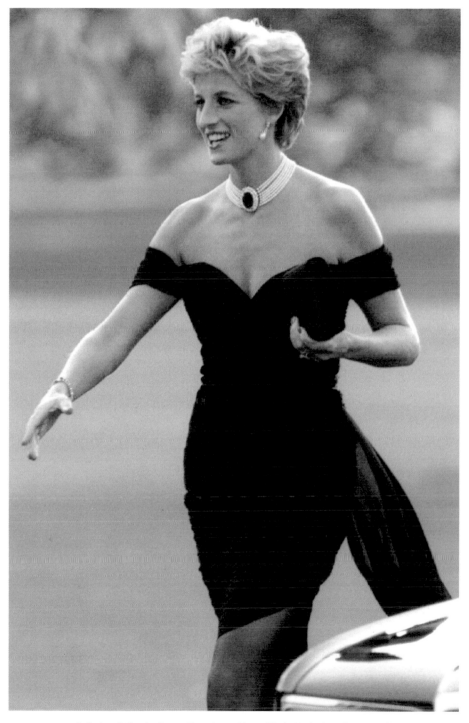

Left, Ayer's Rock, Australia, 1983. *Above*, Hyde Park, London, 1994.

The oldest unmarried Prince of Wales in British history, Charles entered his thirties in 1978 under considerable pressure from his parents and future subjects to find himself a bride. To him, there seemed no great urgency: his mother was still in the prime of life, with two other sons to guarantee the succession. Throughout his twenties, as he explored the world via stints in all three armed services, he had enjoyed a succession of romances with girls both suitable and less so. Some eligible English roses, even the latest generation of the aristocracy, were modern enough career girls not to want to be Queen of England. Others, especially those with what the British like to euphemise as a "past", fell by the wayside after lurid publicity. One of his particular favourites, Camilla Shand, was not deemed blue-blooded enough to be a future consort; Charles dithered so long that she gave up on him, and married one of his polo-playing friends, Andrew Parker-Bowles.

By the time he met Diana again, the ranks of eligible brides had grown rather thin. "You'd better get on with it," his father would say, "or there won't be anyone left." After the murder of his great-uncle, Lord Mountbatten, by the IRA in 1980, Charles found himself touched by young Diana's tender offers of comfort. "You poor thing," she said to him, "you looked so miserable at the funeral. You need someone to look after you."

If she did not exactly throw herself at Charles, as some suggested at the time, Diana was certainly in awe of him, yearning to fall headlong in love. For his part, she fitted all the royal specifications: young, blue-blooded, beautiful and above all a virgin. This antique requirement of the House of Windsor was even verified at a press conference by Diana's uncle. Through the winter of 1980 Charles agonised; in early 1981 he proposed, she accepted and their engagement was announced; and that July they were married in St Paul's Cathedral in front of 700 million people, amid scenes of national rejoicing which lent the monarchy an entirely new lease on life.

When an heir was born within a year, and a "spare" (as they say in royal circles) two years later, Diana was again fulfilling the Archbishop of Canterbury's pledge that this marriage would prove "the stuff of fairy tales". Already she was an international superstar of an order unprecedented in the House of Windsor, a glamorous cover-girl whose face sold out magazines the world over. The demure kindergarten teacher of her first public appearances, blushing as she played good-humoured hide-and-seek with photographers, soon became a more confident-looking fashion plate, beloved of the world's leading designers. Behind the stylish and glamorous facade, however, lay continuing doubts and uncertainties, a fundamental lack of self-esteem, even self-belief, which was to haunt her all her life.

From her first public night out as Britain's future Queen, daringly décolletée for a meeting with Princess Grace of Monaco, Diana sent out signals that she was determined to be different, to forge a new style of royalty more in touch with the times. Her personal style was refreshingly informal, and she was

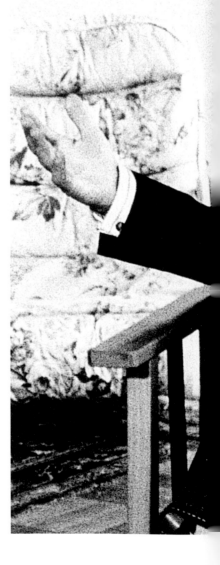

The first television interview, 1981.

48

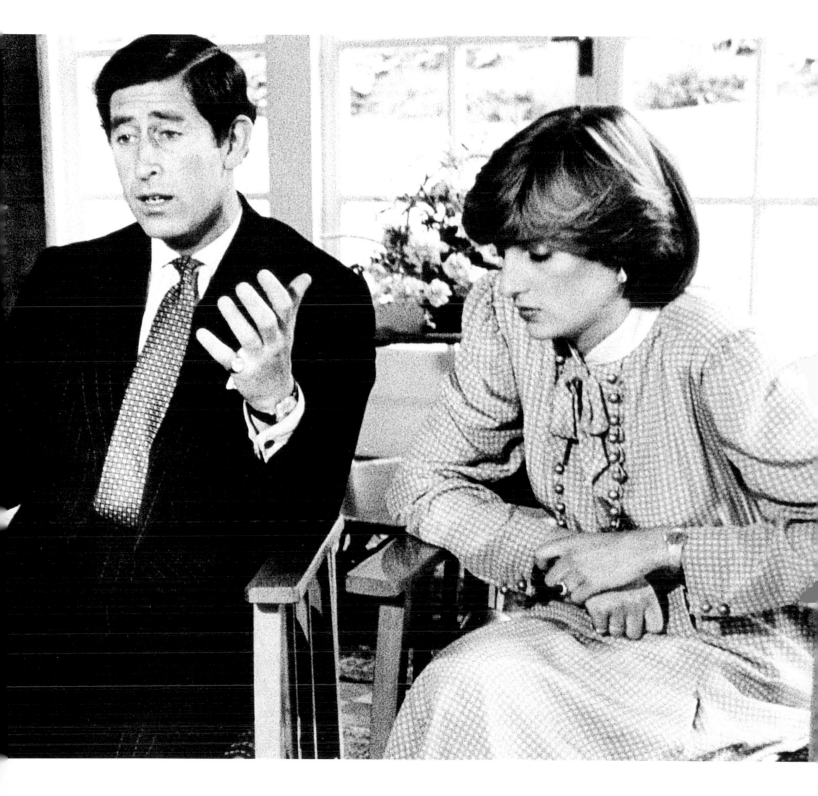

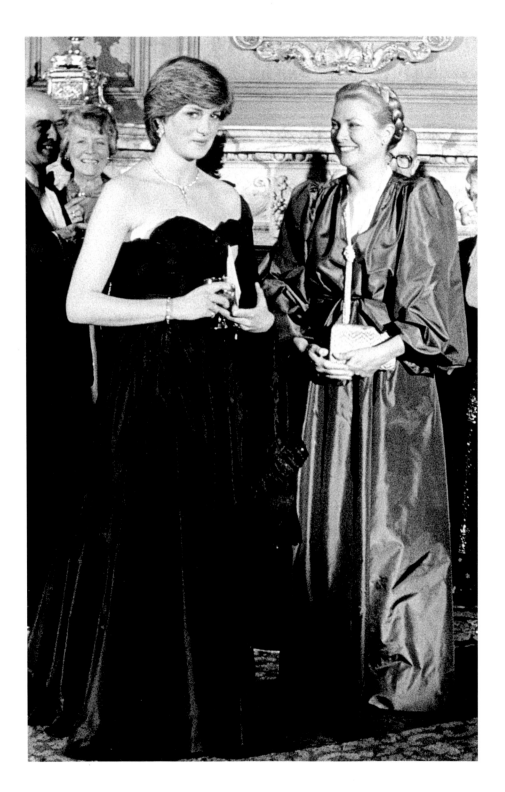

Left, with Princess Grace
of Monaco, 1981.

Right, with the Duchess
of York at Ascot, 1992.

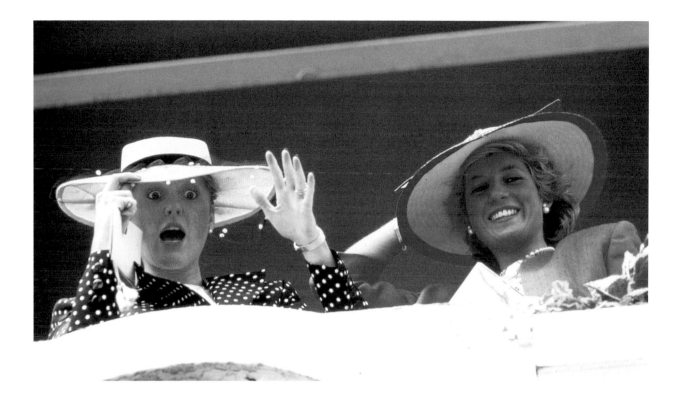

universally loved for it. She even retained the affection of young women her own age, whose private dreams she had stolen, while metamorphosing from the princess-next-door, wearing off-the-peg chain-store clothes with personal adornments, to a Walt Disney princess wearing glamorous gowns few other girls could afford.

By the mid-1980s, joined in the royal circle by her friend Sarah Ferguson, now the Duchess of York, Diana had become the world's most photographed woman. To some, she was merely famous because of the man she married, a spoilt little rich girl up to childish pranks with her friend "Fergie". It was to be some time yet before feminists could warm to Diana any more than traditional royalists, dehumanised by protocol. To most, however, she was a delightful adornment to the universal family – everyone's daughter, everyone's sister, bringing some sparkle into humdrum lives.

Though at first pleased to be relieved of the spotlight, Charles soon grew visibly uneasy. "I'm sorry there aren't two Dianas," he would say, smiling through clenched teeth, to crowds who groaned when their side got him instead of her. Accustomed since birth to being the centre of universal attention, it was not easy for the sometime "playboy prince" to accept second place in the popularity polls to a young, inexperienced wife with an instinct for the common touch. When he made what he considered an important speech, all the press reported next day was his wife's new hat or hairstyle. So he stopped taking her with him.

Thus was born the "PoW, or Prisoner of Wales", as she came to call herself. For longer than she or the nation wanted, Charles and his advisers wrapped their trump card in cotton-wool, refusing to allow her to make speeches – partly because they underestimated her intelligence, and partly for fear that, like a silent movie star transferring to the talkies, she would shatter the illusion by opening her mouth.

How wrong they were. At a time when HIV first made its grim presence felt around the world, Diana's innate sense of fellow-feeling pioneered a quantum leap in the potent symbolism available to royalty. By shaking hands with a dying AIDS patient, having first conspicuously removed her glove, she did a great deal to dispel public prejudice and fear – far more, to be sure, than a multi-million-pound government advertising campaign of the time warning cryptically: "Don't die of ignorance."

Leaks from Buckingham Palace made it clear that the "born" royals did not regard AIDS as a seemly cause for royal patronage. This was perhaps the moment at which Diana's sense of self began to take clearer shape. Impatient with the stuffy rules of royal life, bored with the cold formality of the world behind Palace walls, unable to shed her natural sense of fun and spontaneity, she began to find her own identity by boldly reinventing the art of being royal. Already she had defied the rule book with such popular innovations as taking her infant son with her on an official visit to Australia. Now her informal style became her trademark, setting her conspicuously apart from her in-laws. At Balmoral, her mother-in-law's Scottish castle, she shut out the royal world behind the gold-plated headphones of her Walkman.

But Diana was meanwhile doing much more than her duty. Abroad, she made Britain seem glamorous again. On tours of the Commonwealth, trips to America, the Middle East and India, from Africa to Japan, she reawakened interest in a distant monarchy which increasingly looked a cobwebbed relic of the past. Her ability to make direct contact with the humblest people, as if they were the most important in the world, combined with her sparkling eyes and luminous smile to make Charles seem stiff and awkward. There had always been concern about the thirteen-year age gap between them, their different interests and enthusiasms, their different circles of friends. The marriage began to founder long before the public realised. When tell-tale signs became evident in their body language, often the only source of access to true royal feelings, devotees of the fairy tale still refused to believe it.

When Diana's unhappiness was finally chronicled in vivid detail, with stark revelations of eating disorders, even suicide attempts, a disbelieving public turned on the media, trying to blame the messenger for the message. But Diana herself offered no dissent (and was later revealed to have authorised the details). There was an ugly period of public relations warfare, when she and her husband used press leaks via "friends" to fight their private battles in public. At the end of 1992, the Queen's "annus horribilis", a formal separation had become

Opposite, above, Korea, 1992, with the prime minister, Hyun Soong.

Below, tour of Canada, 1987.

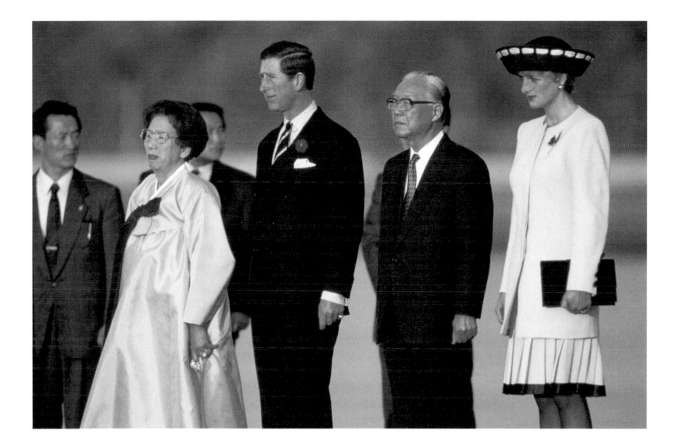

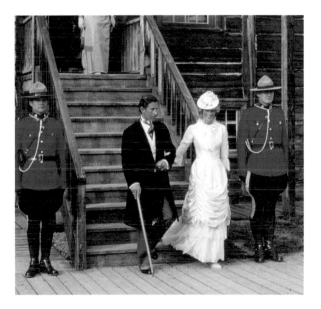

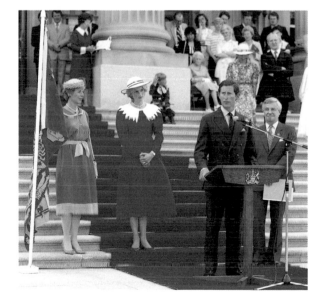

inevitable. After Prime Minister John Major confirmed the news in the House of Commons, his predecessor Edward Heath rose to call it "the saddest announcement by a prime minister in modern times".

Divorce was unthinkable, insisted the Palace – as did Diana, still haunted by that of her own parents. Through four uncomfortable years, until it was finalised in August 1996, she continued to insist that she never wanted a divorce. But there had been "three in the marriage", and Charles might want to start a new life. When Diana's rival for her husband's affections appeared in public, she was pelted with bread rolls by fellow-housewives at their local supermarket. So unassailable was Diana's public popularity that Camilla Parker-Bowles, despite maintaining a dignified silence as her own marriage also ended, became the most hated woman in the land.

Again, Diana had been cheated of the happy domesticity she had always craved. Her whole life, she would say to friends, had been a series of betrayals. Nor would it be easy to rebuild. As the mother of the future king, she faced huge obstacles to finding a new family life, perhaps having the daughters she always wanted. Only at the very end of her life, in those last few weeks when she was still causing daily surprises, did she appear at last to find happiness in the arms of Dodi Fayed, son of the controversial Egyptian immigrant who admired Britain enough to buy two of its most venerable totems, Harrods department store and *Punch* magazine, as well as a London football club.

A successful film producer, with an Oscar to his name for *Chariots of Fire*, Dodi offered Diana the respect and affection she had always been denied by those from whom she most needed it, if not by her legion of admirers. His father had long been friends with hers; the Fayeds were a family large, warm and rich enough to ring-fence her with feelings of security, to make her at last feel loved, needed, appreciated. They liked her for herself, not just her status and renown.

So happy was Diana in those last few weeks, as she told many friends, that there were none of the usual complaints when paparazzi pictures of her and Dodi eclipsed coverage of her trip to Bosnia as part of her gritty campaign for a global ban on landmines. The day before they died together, they exchanged significant gifts. She gave him silver cufflinks which had once been her father's. He gave her a diamond ring and a silver plaque inscribed with a poem. It was found under her pillow in his apartment, the intended destination of their last ride together, when the sharp incline down to a Paris underpass became a descent into Hades.

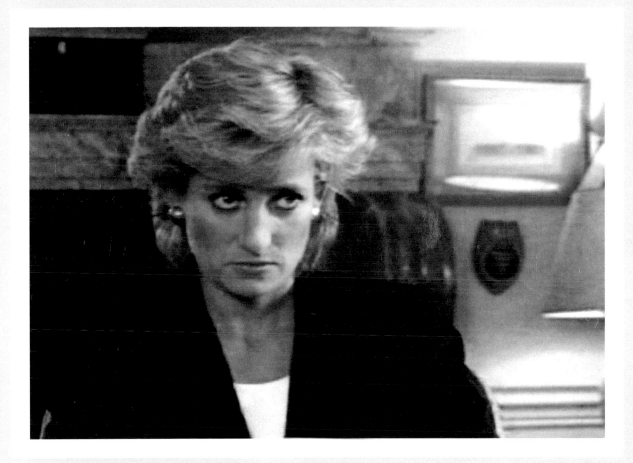

"There were three of us in the marriage, so it was a bit crowded."

MOTHERHOOD

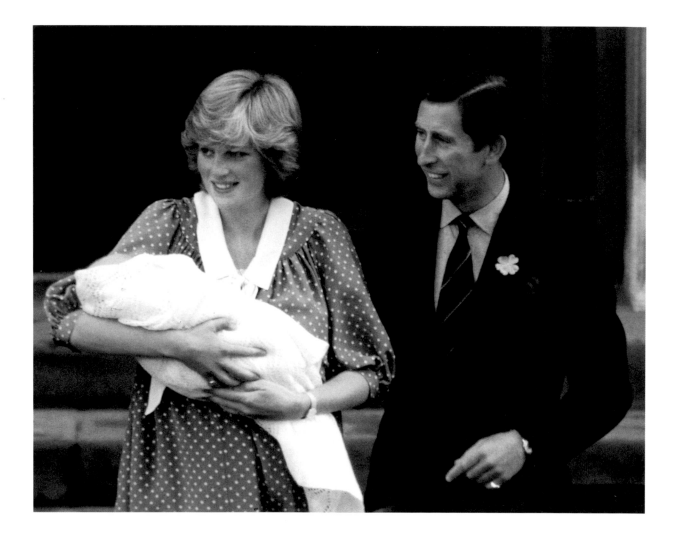

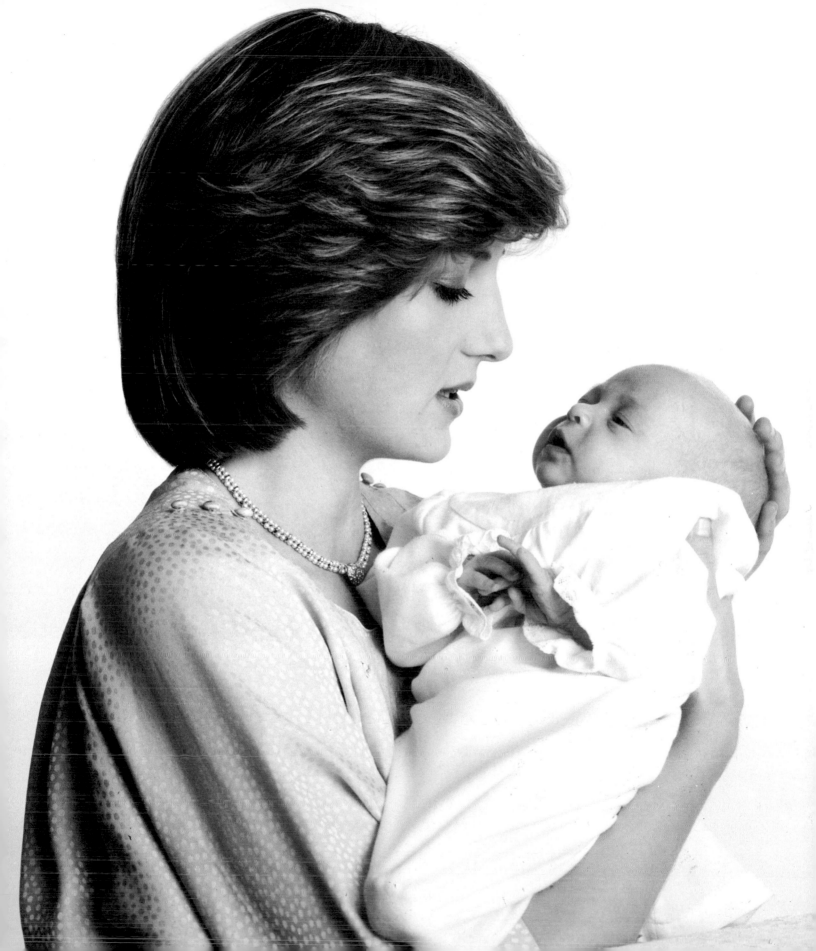

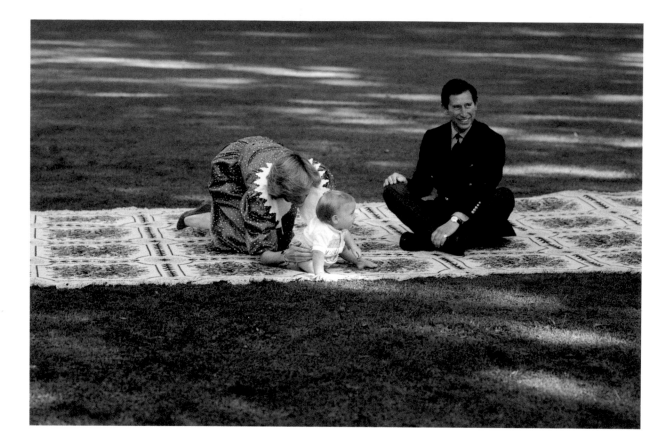

Above, New Zealand, 1983.

Opposite, photographed
by Snowdon with Prince
Harry, 1984.

"It is a tribute to her level-headedness and
strength that despite the most bizarre life
imaginable after her childhood she remained
intact, true to herself."

— THE EARL SPENCER

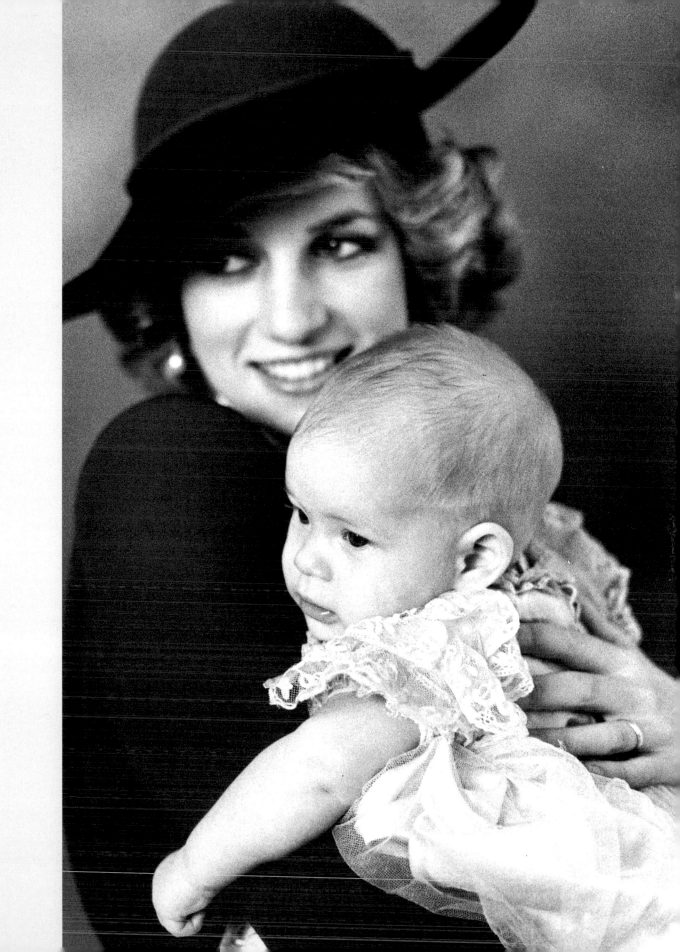

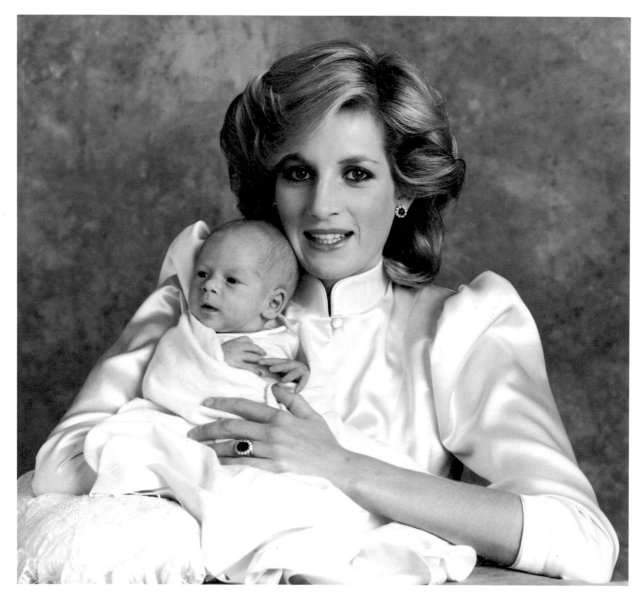

Prince Harry was born on 15 September 1984.

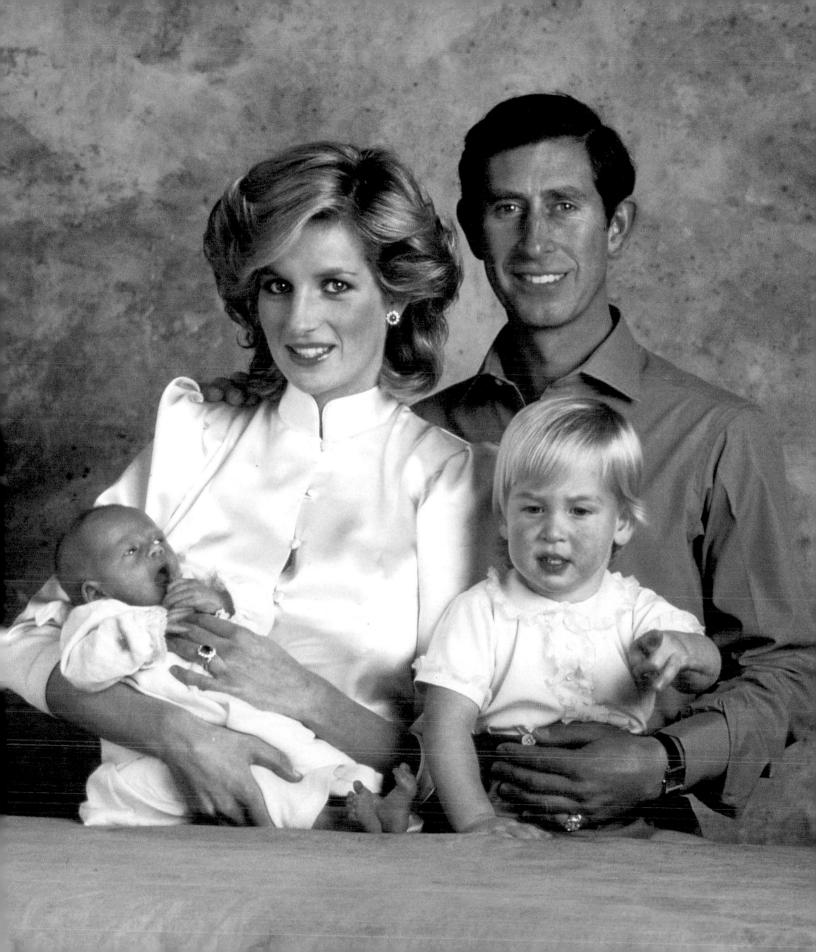

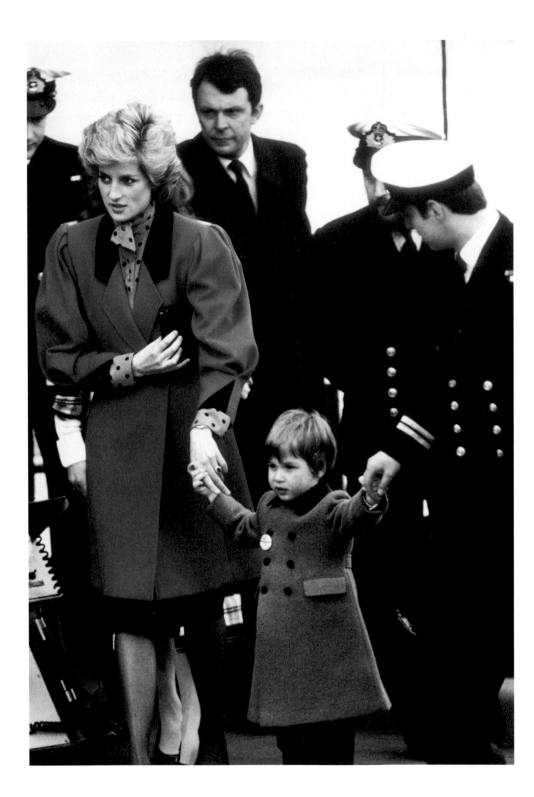

Showing Prince
William around his
uncle's warship,
1985.

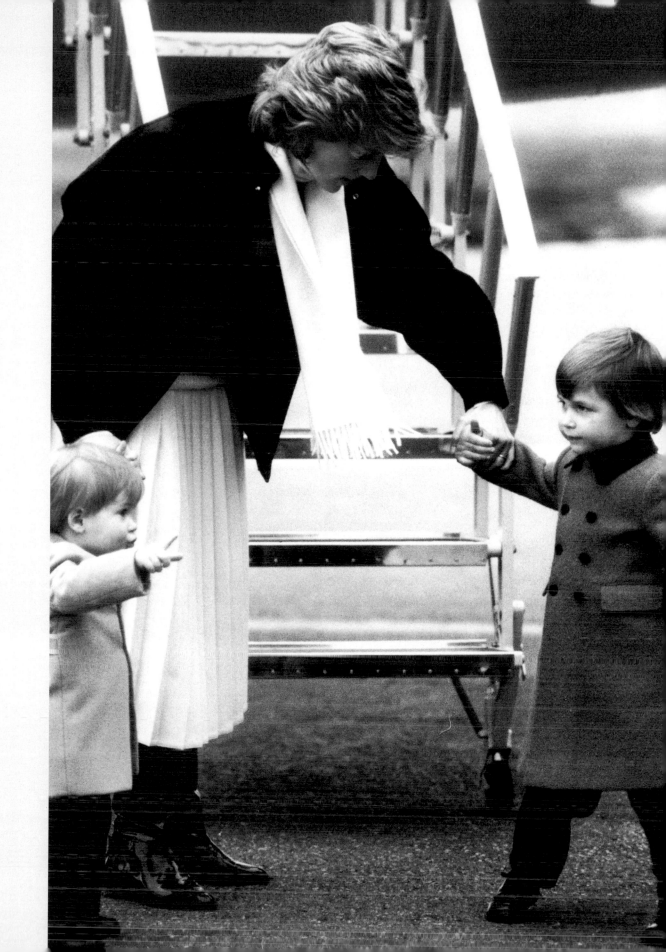

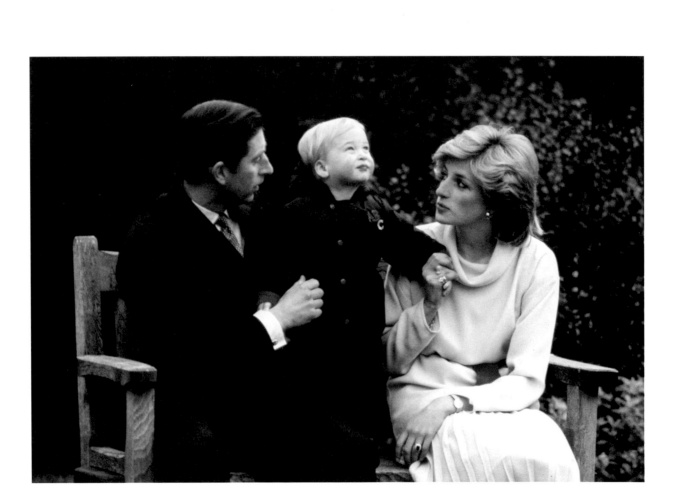

Above, Kensington Palace, 1984. *Right*, school sports day, June 1990.

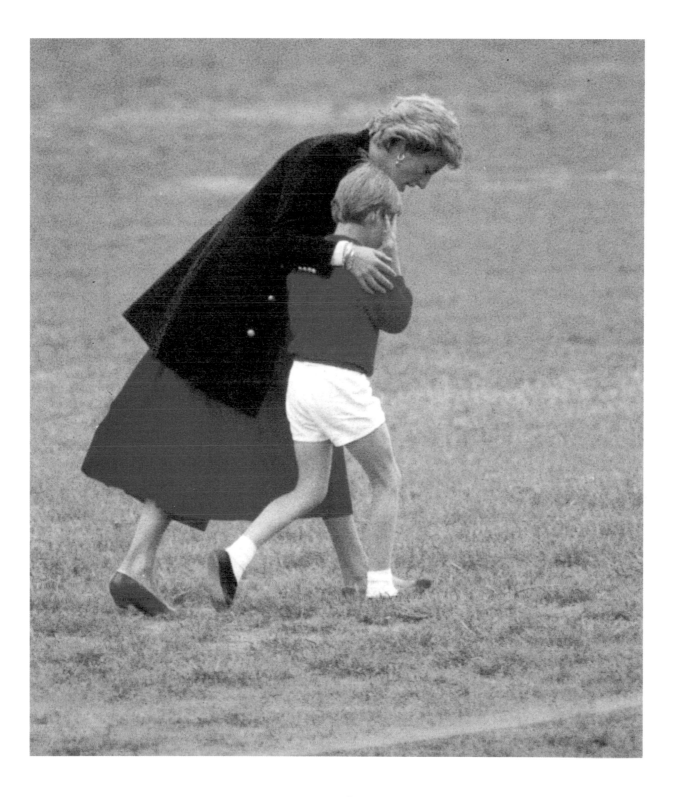

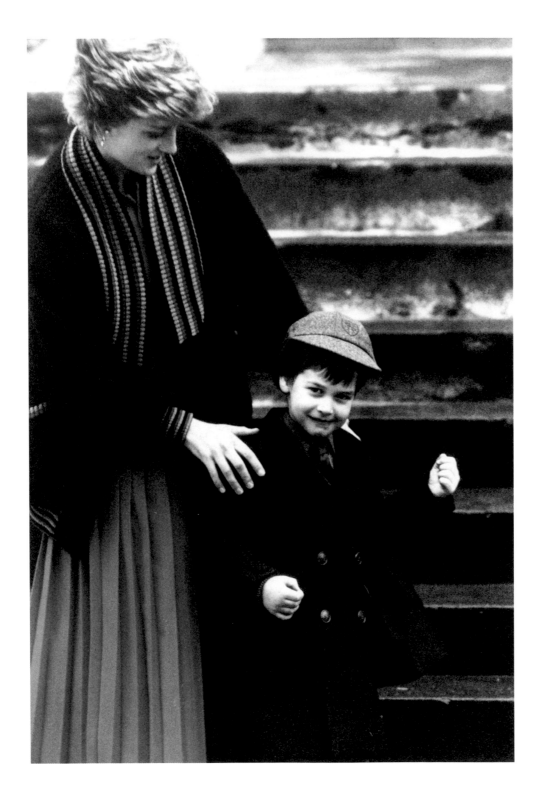

First days at school,
1988 and 1989.

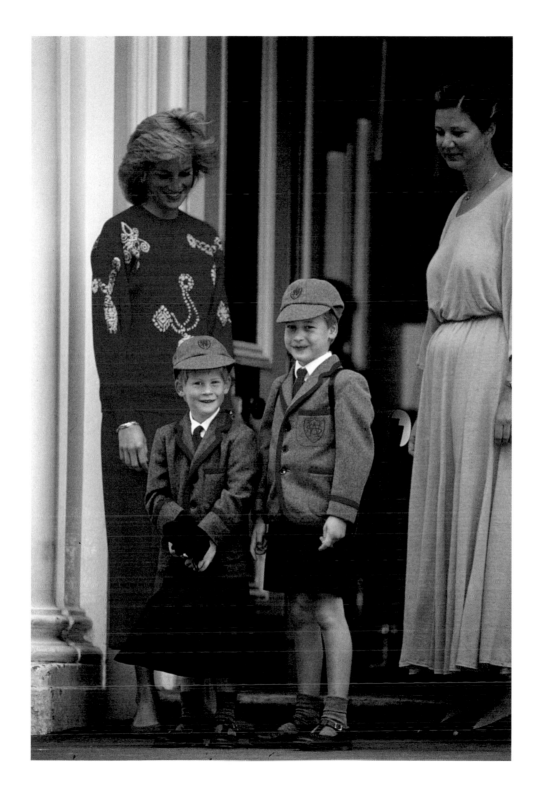

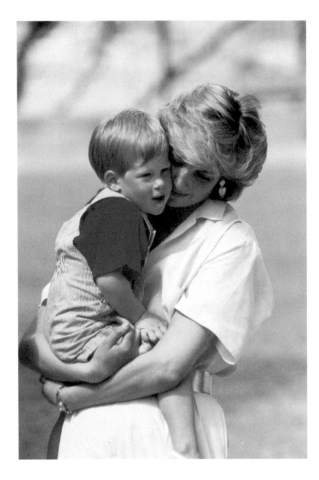

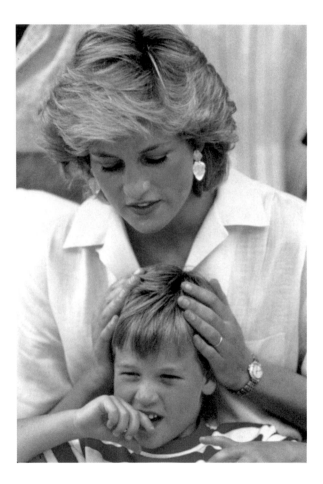

Majorca, 1987.

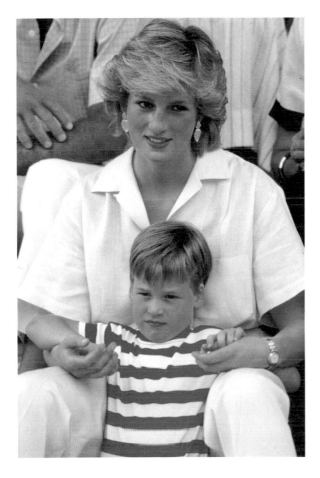

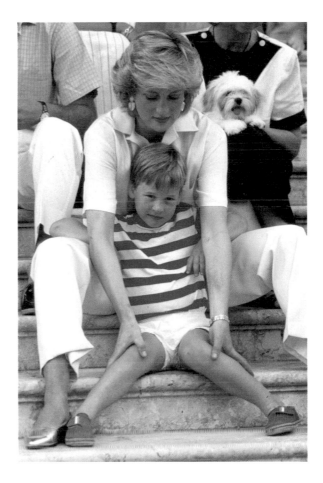

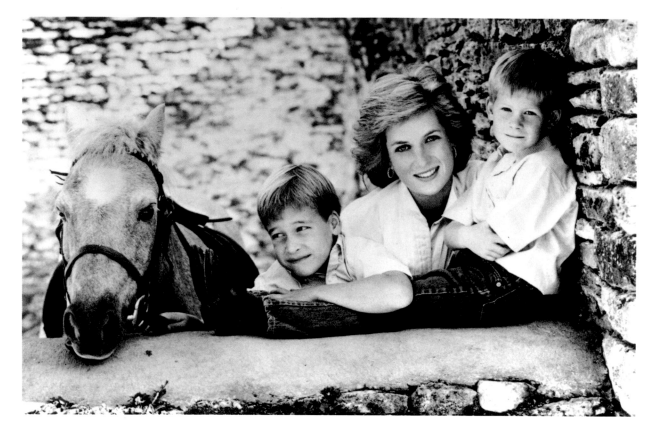

Highgrove, 1990.
Opposite, Prince Harry.

"I always feed my children
love and affection – it's so
important.... They mean
everything to me."

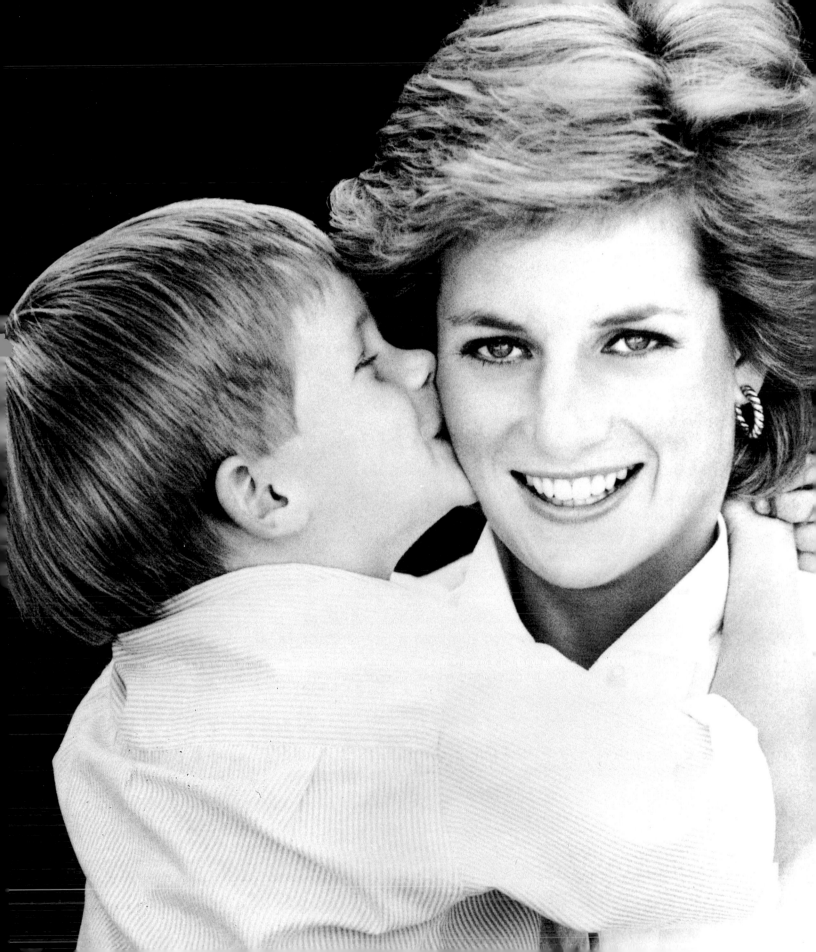

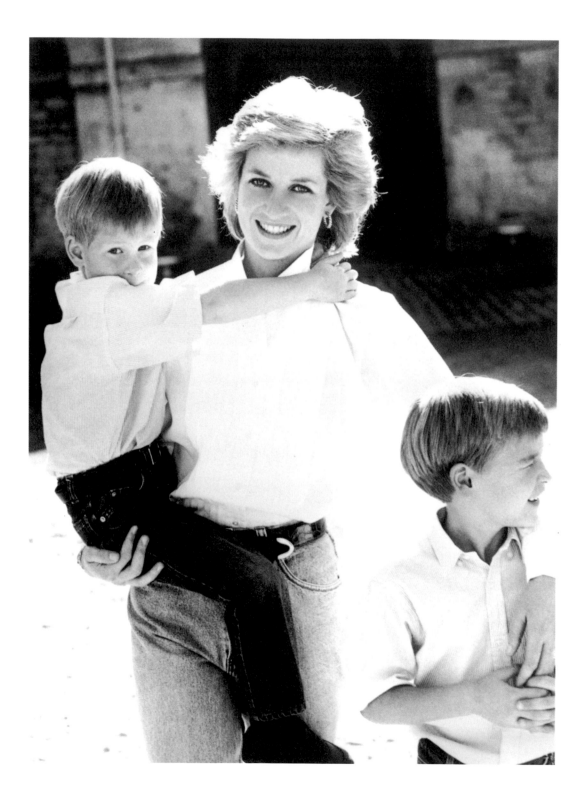

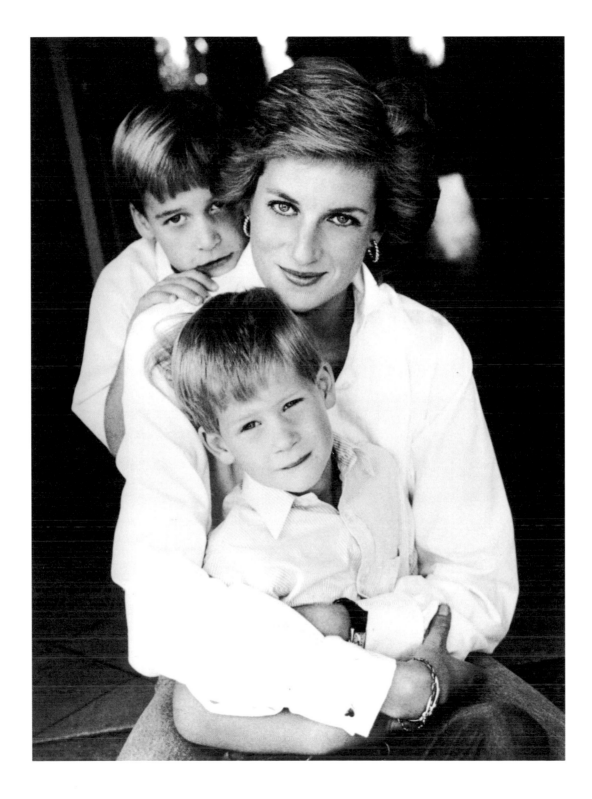

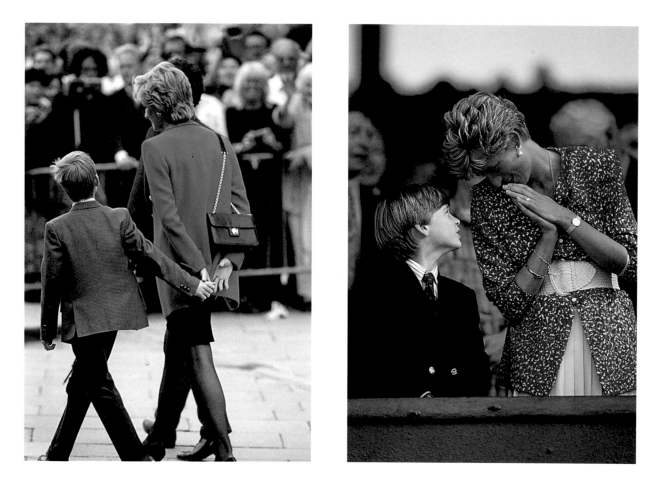

Left, Prince William's first day at Eton, 1995. *Right*, Wimbledon, 1991. *Opposite*, Venice, 1985.

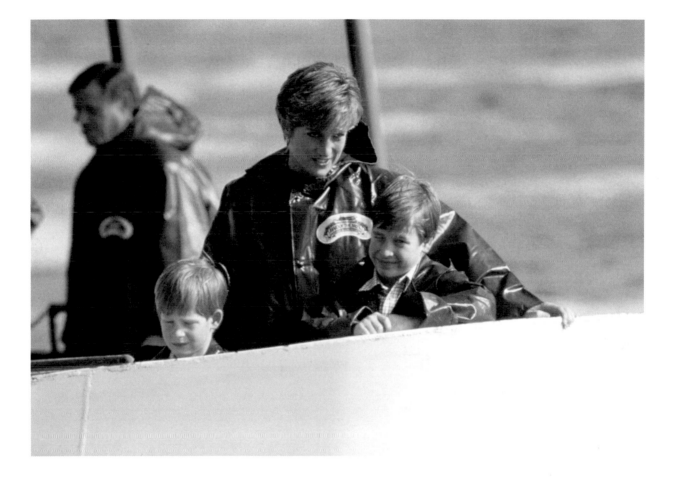

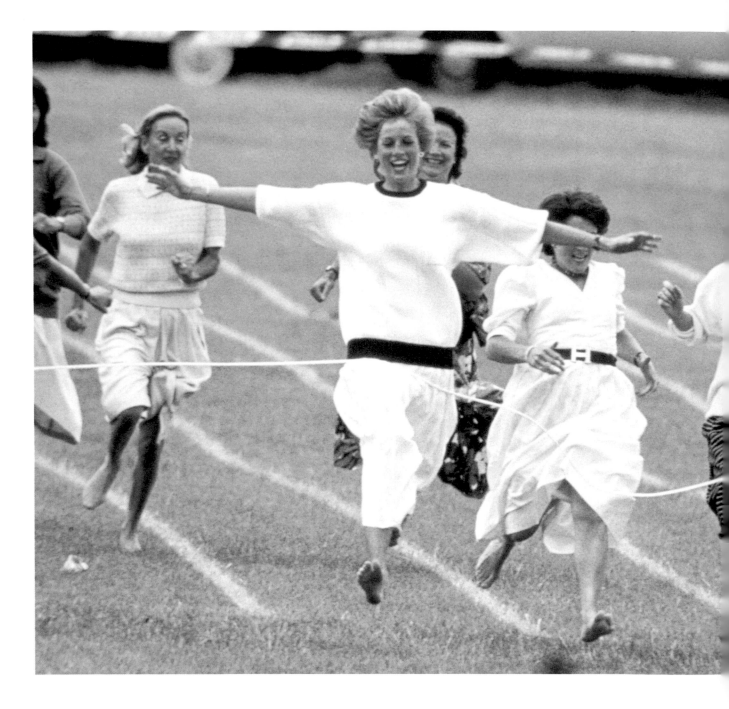

Above, mothers' race at the school sports day, June 1989. *Right*, visits to Thorpe Park, 1992 and 1993.

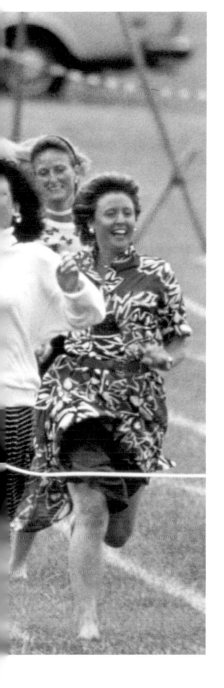

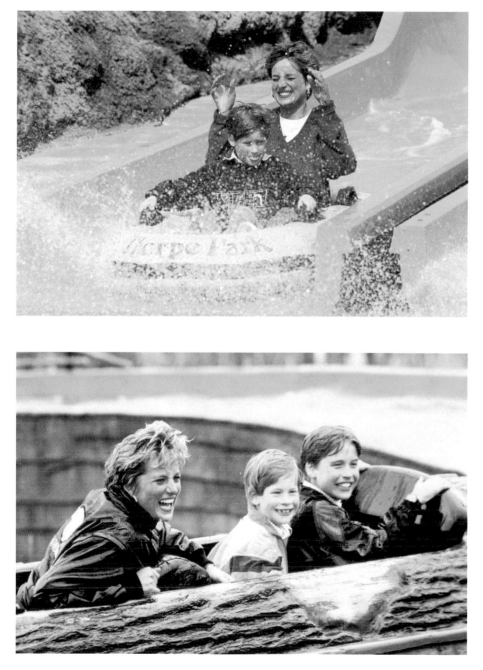

REACHING OUT

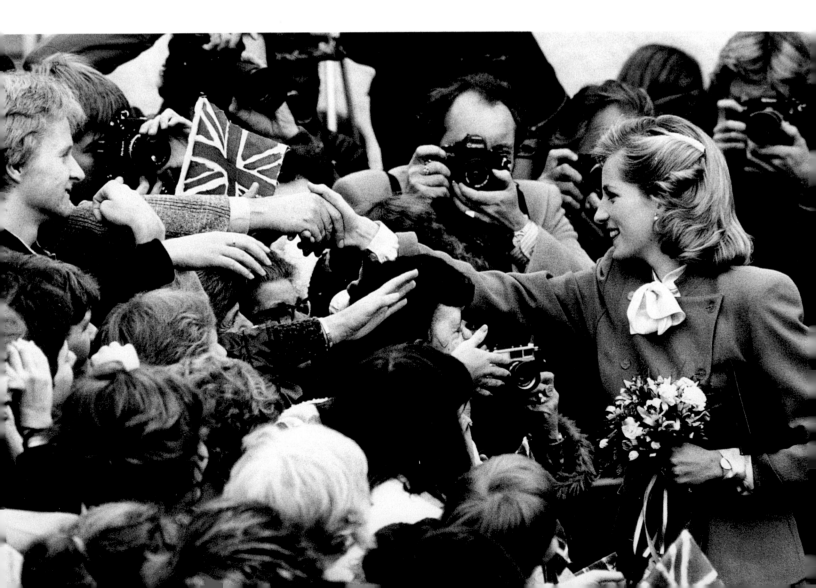

"I love being with people."

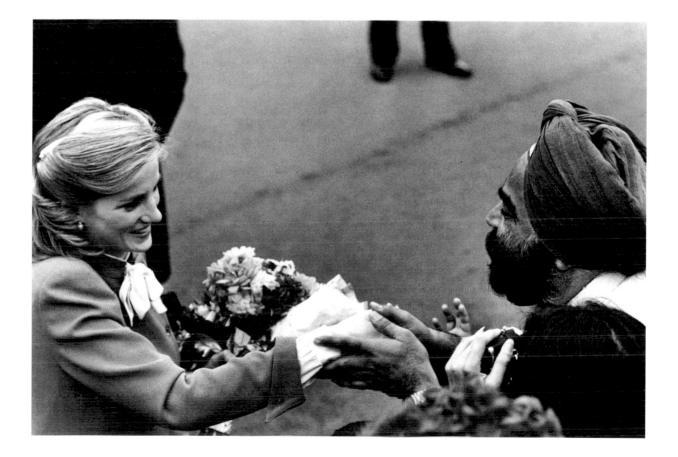

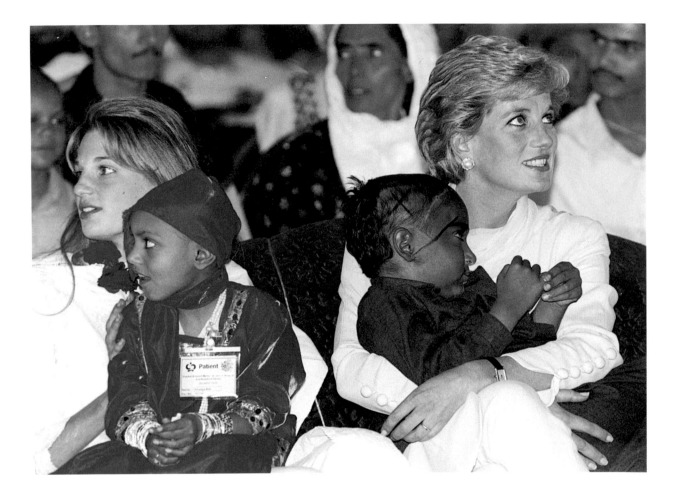

Lahore, 1996.

"Anywhere I see suffering is
where I want to be, doing
what I can."

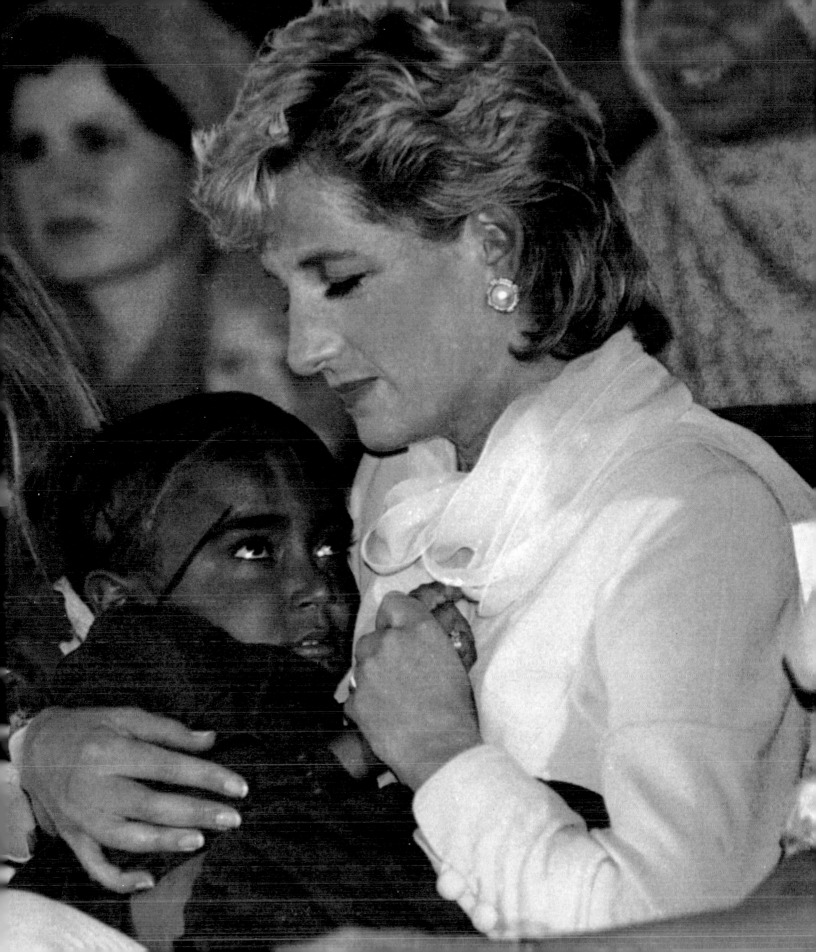

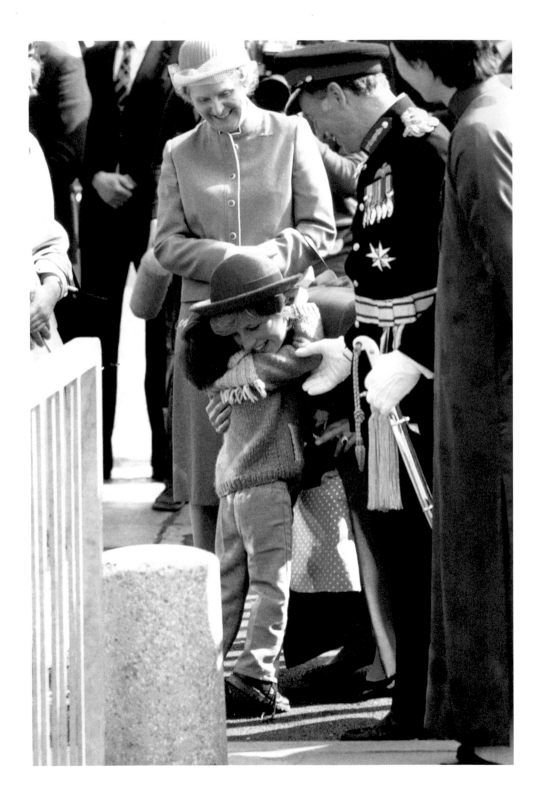

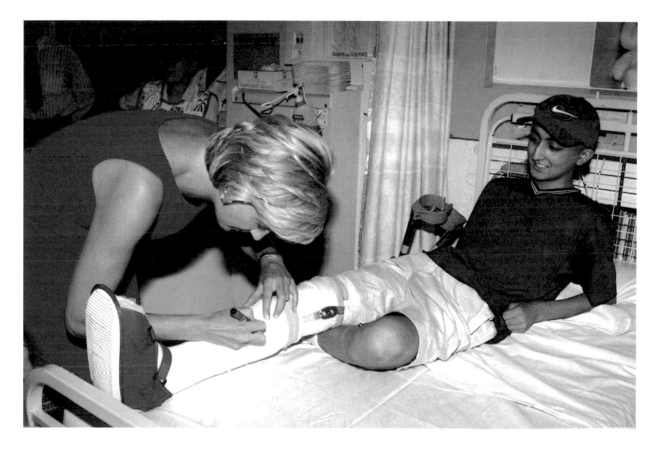

Opposite, Liverpool, 1982. *Above*, Northwick Park Hospital, London, 1997.

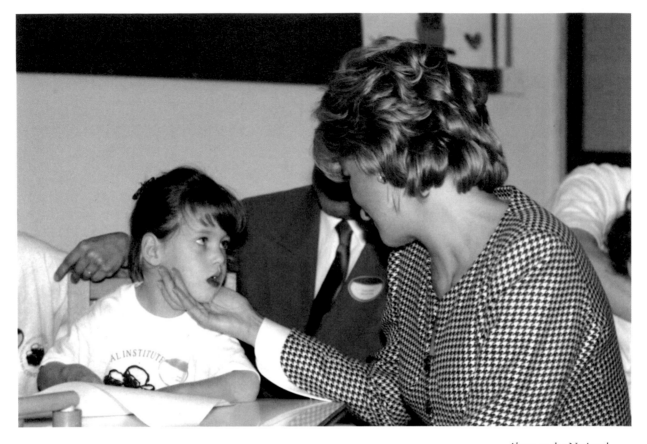

Above, at the National
Institute of Conductive
Education, 1995.

Opposite, Moscow
Children's Hospital, 1995.

"Diana told me about the
importance of touch: of how
just cupping her hands round
someone's face gave huge
comfort, and transcended all
barriers of race and language."
— ROSA MONCKTON

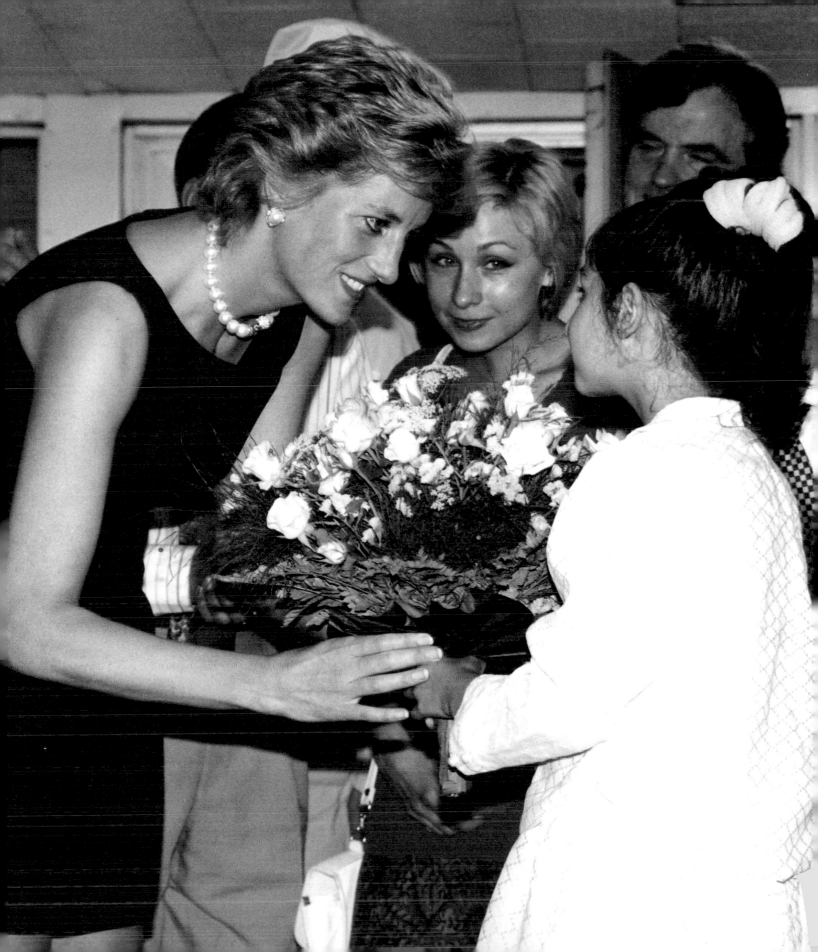

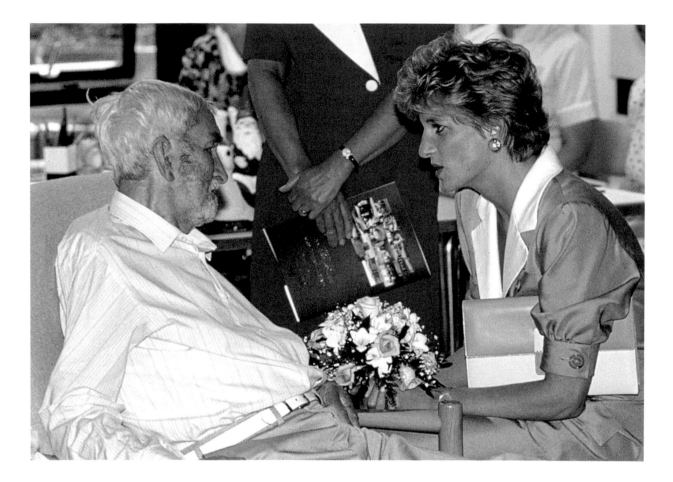

Above, Trinity Hospice, Blackpool, 1992.

Opposite, Harare, Zimbabwe, 1993.

Overleaf, an AIDS patient in Brazil, 1991.

"The biggest disease this world suffers from is the disease of people feeling unloved. I know that I can give love, for a minute, for half an hour, for a day, for a week."

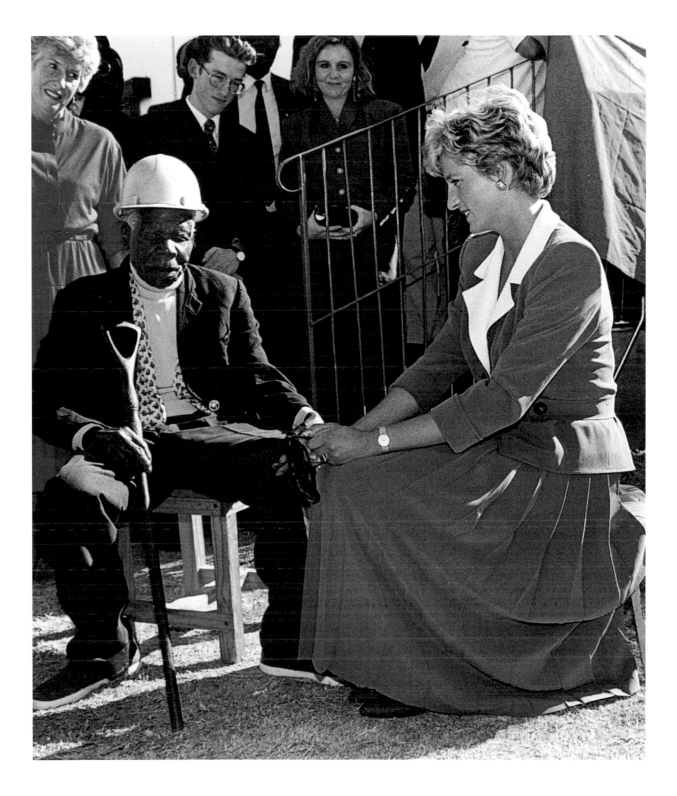

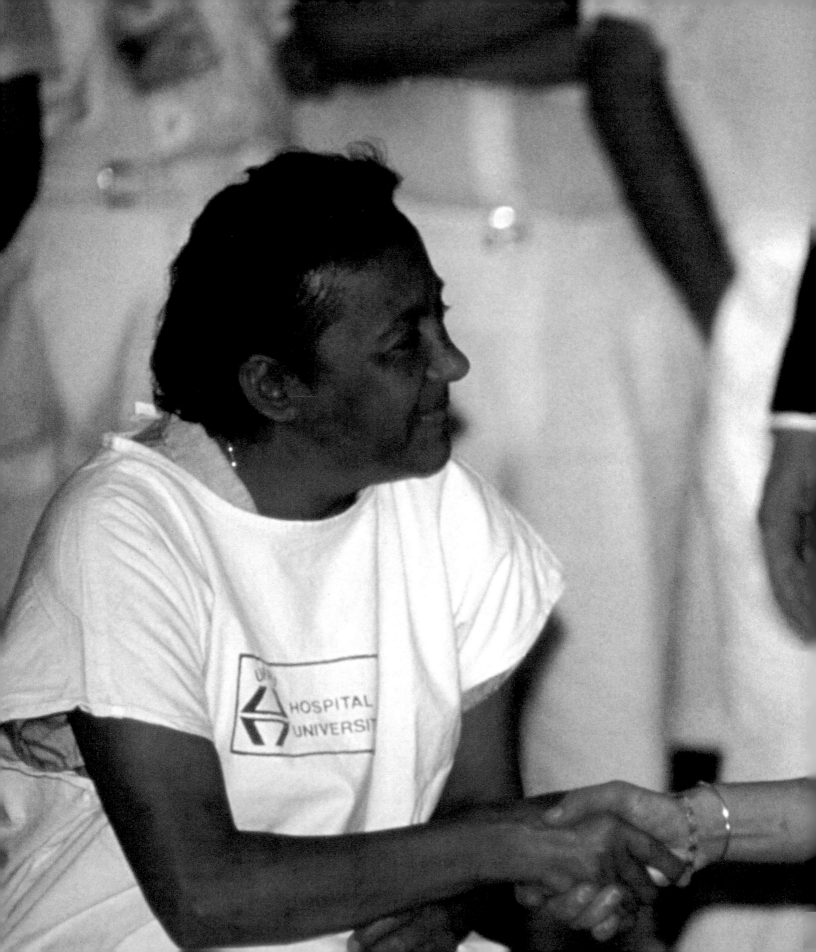

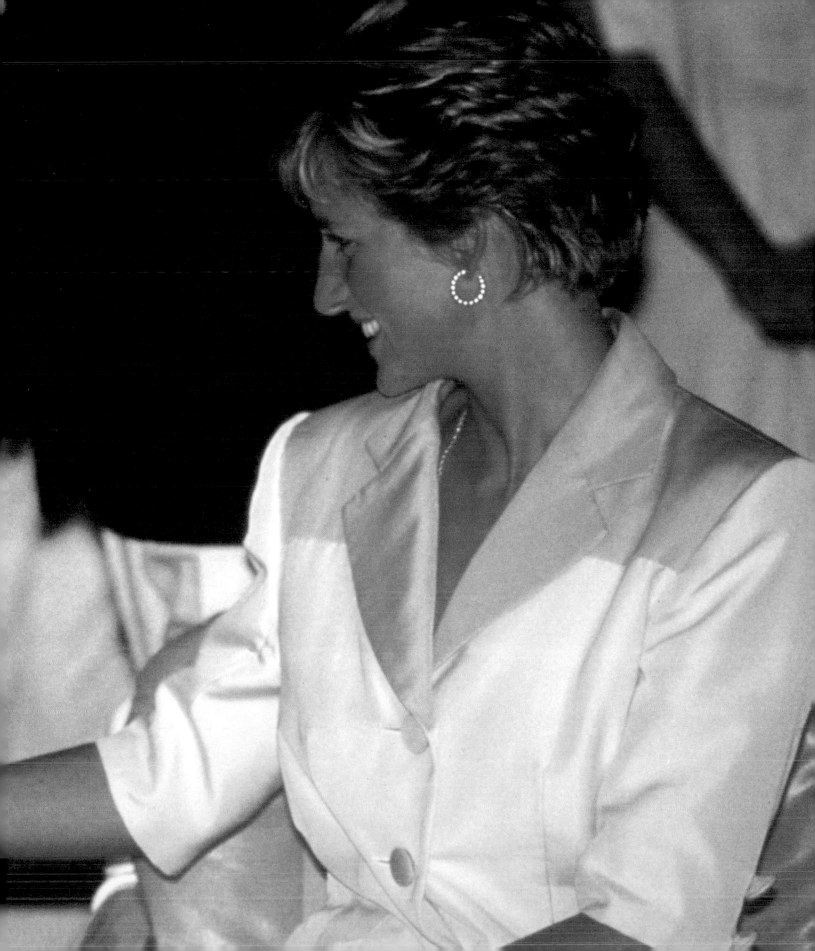

Nine months before her death, when there was no one else around to overhear, I asked Diana what kind of man might one day tempt her to remarry. Without a moment's hesitation, she replied: "Someone who understands what I'm about." Which gave me the chance to ask: "So what *are* you about?"

"I'm about caring," she replied, leaning forward with a sudden intensity in those spellbinding eyes. "I always have been, and I always will be. I thought I had married one caring man, but alas it didn't work out. Perhaps one day I will meet another." It reads almost like self-caricature, but it didn't sound that way at the time. Diana was in deadly earnest.

I had first met her, like a thousand other journalists, as the "shy Di" who beguiled and flirted with the world in the months leading up to her engagement and marriage. I was her husband's biographer, commissioned to update for his fortieth birthday a book I had published on his thirtieth. So much was Diana to change Charles during that decade, however, that an entirely new book was eventually called for. Marriage to a devoted young woman, who swiftly blessed him with two sons, liberated the prince at last from the long shadow of his parents, bringing out his softer, feminine side, his own capacity for compassion and concern.

The pity was that he could not find a way to extend that compassion to a wife with problems of her own, that concern to a woman afflicted by the eating disorder *bulimia nervosa*. Freed to explore his interest in matters spiritual, Charles was lampooned as the "loony" prince who talked to his plants and wandered the Kalahari desert with an elderly Jungian guru. It was far from fair; but it added to the tensions within the marriage. Himself prone to a depressive streak, the prince was not equipped by his coldly formal upbringing to understand Diana's difficulties, let alone help her with them. He was too set in his bachelor ways, too much of the old school, to change – too busy trying to be a "modern" prince to become a "new age" husband. In one of the greatest ironies of her short life, the Queen of Hearts' husband chose to seek his own solace elsewhere.

Come the separation and divorce, observers like myself were reluctantly forced to take sides, as is so often the case when personal friends go their separate ways. Seeing Diana as the victim, undervalued and maltreated by a man whose character I knew better than most, I was among the first and the most consistent to defend her in print against the continual assaults of what she called "the enemy", the stream of black propaganda from Buckingham Palace, the crude insults from "friends" of Prince Charles, the relentless vilification she received from a sceptical press. "She never understood," as her brother Charles put it at her funeral, "why her genuinely good intentions were sneered at by the media, why there appeared to be a permanent quest to bring her down."

For fifteen years I had been an unofficial public relations man for her husband – better, I often thought to myself, than the ones he actually paid – whose public work in the shape of the Prince's Trust, helping disadvantaged youth into employment, otherwise received less credit than was its due. It was

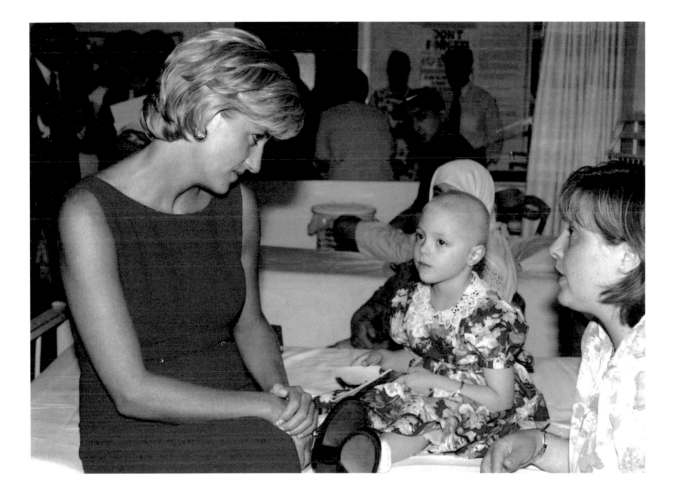

Northwick Park Hospital, London, 1997.

not Charles's way to offer thanks, nor did I really expect any. So when Diana made indirect approaches about meeting up – a course, at that time of domestic warfare, fraught with danger for her – I was pleasantly surprised. When I was warmly thanked for my support through dark and difficult times, I could see at once why the "born" royals would find her human qualities so threatening.

Over her last five years, there was a series of "coincidental" meetings in London restaurants, when she would walk in to find – surprise, surprise – myself and a close mutual friend at the adjacent table. There would be much laughter and many mischievous looks as the meals began separately, the joint was checked for other journalists, and then the two tables were hooked up. Once she brought the boys; once she was with her mother, with whom relations had recently been repaired. Diana was giggling because she had been invited to accept some obscure-sounding dental award in Australia. "I've got these amazing teeth, apparently," she laughed, flashing them dazzlingly. "But I owe them all to her."

That day she was full of a recent trip to New York, when she had stayed alone in a hotel room for the first time in her life. Settling into the Carlyle Hotel, and discovering the joys of room service – with no one, for once, to tell her what not to do – she was surprised to hear the telephone ring. No one knew she was there. "Is this Lady Diana?" asked the Carlyle switchboard.

"No," said the princess.

"Sorry, Ma'am, is this Princess Di?"

"Yes."

"Well, there's a man on the line says he's your husband. Says his name is Windsor and he's calling from a pay phone down the block."

Realising that some passer-by must have seen her hasty flit from limo to lobby, failed to believe his eyes, and pushed his luck by calling, Diana decided to respond in kind. "So I took the call." They talked for forty minutes, she said, about everything under the sun; and it was typical of her not to give away any more details. Even the confidences of a New York maverick, maybe a hobo, were respected by the outcast maverick of the House of Windsor.

What I loved about this story, and said so, was the thought of this guy – be he hobo or hotshot – diving into the nearest bar to say: "You'll never guess who I've just been talking to" ... only to be greeted by howls of derision. We laughed, as she did with her brother, until we were "bent double".

In October 1996 I was invited to lunch at Kensington Palace. Just the two of us, I was assured: Diana had recently parted company with the press secretary who was for ever disappointing newspaper editors by sitting in on their lunches with her. As I had my best suit pressed, and bought a cheerful new tie, I received another call asking if I would mind postponing the lunch a few days. Something had come up. She just hated to do this, and would explain all when I saw her.

The following Wednesday I climbed the grand staircase of Kensington Palace, a Mozart piano concerto tinkling in the distance, only to gasp again at her height, grace and beauty as she came bounding out of her sitting room like a designer-clad gazelle. "I'm so sorry about Friday," were her first words, as we

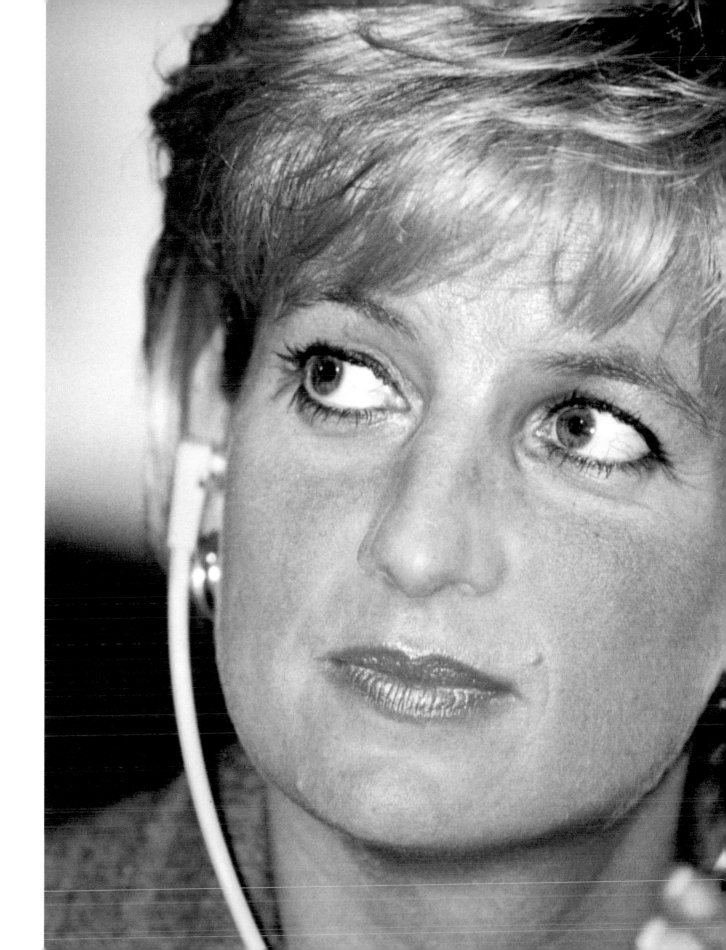

sat down for a pre-prandial drink. "But Magdi Yacoub was performing a heart operation. I had to go."

"How can you stand watching those things?" I said light-heartedly. "All that blood. I'm sure I would keel over."

For once, she didn't smile back. "If I am to care for people in hospital," she replied, leaning forward with ferocious intensity, "I need to know every aspect of the long treatment they have been through." There was never any doubting her sincerity. "Caring" was topic number one almost as soon as we had shaken hands.

Over the ensuing two hours our conversation roamed all over the world, from affectionate intimacies about people in both our lives to vignettes of world leaders both admiring and irreverent. In private she was utterly disarming, very funny, with an infectious laugh and a deft line in repartee. Diana was no giant intellect, as she well knew, but she was smart, savvy and interested in weightier subjects than she was given credit for. Throughout that lunch, however, two themes kept recurring: her public work and her children. She was worried that Harry would get left out of things; all the girls would go for William. She was bringing up Harry as a support system for his brother in the trials that lay ahead. Whatever her other preoccupations – a delegation was due at 3 pm to beg her to go to Thailand – those boys remained the still centre of Diana's turning world.

Four years before, my wife had enjoyed a secret lunch with Diana and two mutual friends – an all-afternoon "girl-talk" session, sharing intimacies none would ever dream of revealing, even now. At the time, as Diana knew, I was writing a book about the royal crisis she had played no small part in precipitating. "What is he going to call it?" Diana asked my wife.

"The Tarnished Crown," she told her.

"Perhaps," laughed the princess, "it should be called The Tarnished Tiara?"

At her request, I sent her a copy when the book was published. "I couldn't write to thank you," she said later. "You do understand why?" Indeed I did. It was one of the reasons she liked the company of the few others who understood the claustrophobia of life in the royal goldfish bowl. Now I had brought along a copy of my latest book, a biography of Tchaikovsky. She laughed when I urged her not to bother reading it, just leave it lying around for her visitors to see. Within a week of our lunch I received a three-page letter in her bold yet innocent hand, full of articulate detail showing she had read every word. "It brought tears to my eyes," she wrote, as that letter now does to mine.

It was part of the unwritten rules of such meetings that I did not, of course, write about it, and was very careful whom I told. One idle boast in a diary column, and I would never – understandably – be asked again. The few close friends with whom I shared my little Di stories naturally muttered about manipulation. I was putty in her hands; I would never write another rude word about her. But to me, after 25 years in Fleet Street, Diana was no different from any other public figure, least of all the politicians, in trying to establish good relations with trusted writers. At times, it gave her a chance to bounce new ideas

Kensington Palace

October 25th 1996.

Dear Anthony.

I was deeply moved by the account you gave of Tchaikovsky's childhood, infact it brought tears to my eyes . . .

Yours sincerely,

Diana.

off her public; at others, it helped people like me to correct my media brethren's more glaring mistakes. If a political editor lunched privately with the prime minister, he was doing his job, and doing it well; if a royal writer lunched with a princess, it was somehow a cause for concern.

Diana was merely trying to find a constructive way through the piles of garbage written about her over the years. She was doing what I had once urged her ex-husband to do, only to meet a firm rebuff: meet the people who write about you, hold off-the-record background briefings before your major speeches, establish working relationships with editors. At the time, he too was complaining of being "the most misunderstood man in the kingdom". But the remedies I suggested were unthinkable, he said, to royalty.

Not to Diana. She knew her relations with the media were a two-way street, a surrogate romance which was bound to have its ups and downs.

MEDIA

She knew her relations with the

media were a two-way street,

a surrogate romance which

was bound to have its ups

and downs. Photography was

an essential tool of her

public work.

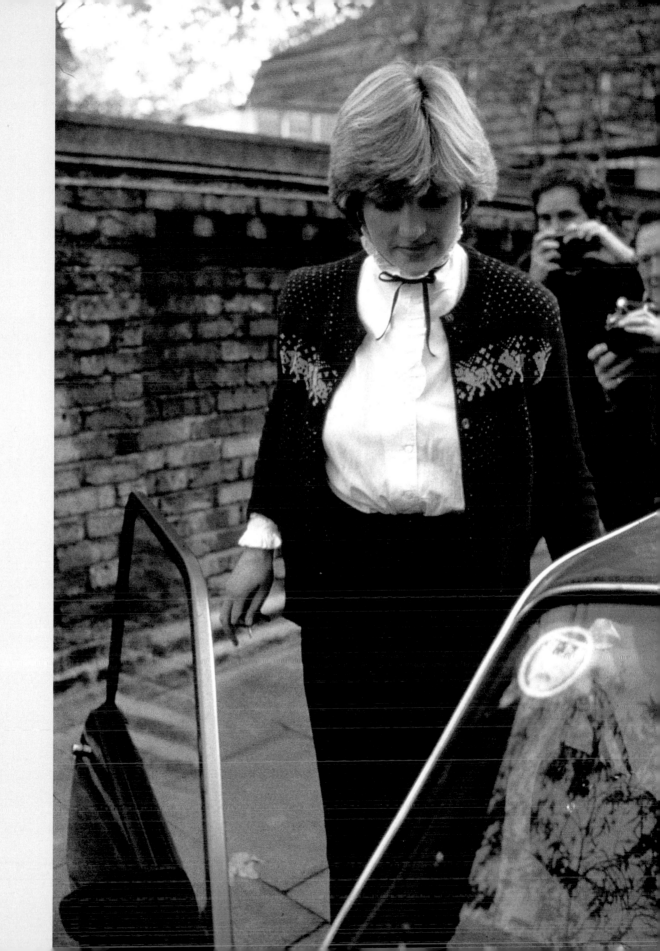

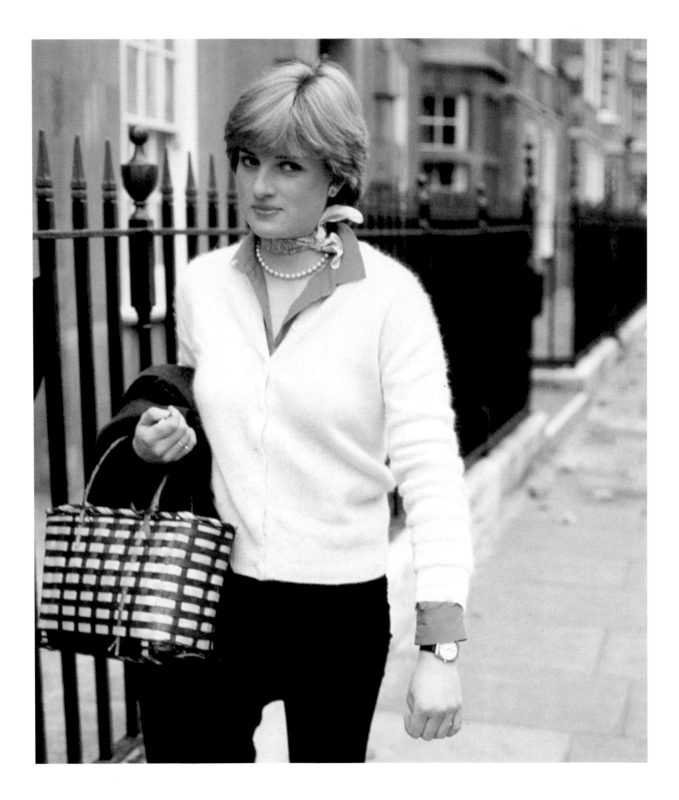

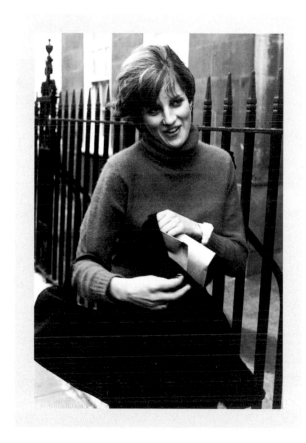

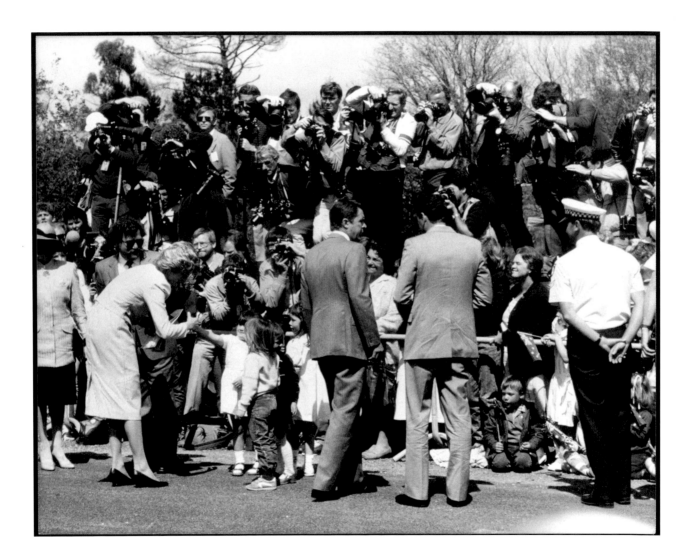

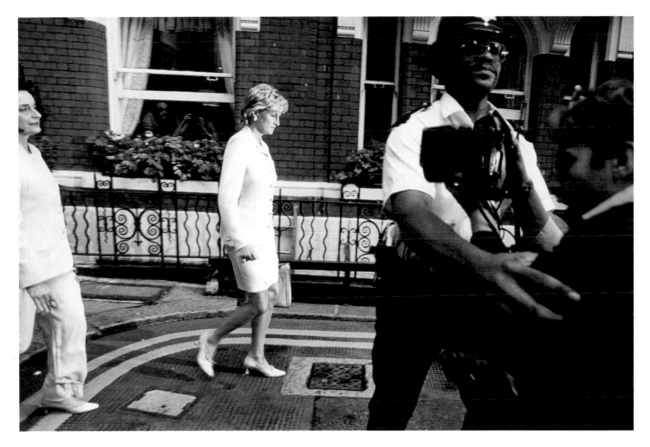

Above, police restrain the photographers, July 1996.

Overleaf, outside the Institute of Contemporary Arts, London, 1993.

"The most daunting aspect was the media attention.... I seemed to be on the front of a newspaper every single day, which is an isolating experience, and the higher the media put you, the bigger the drop."

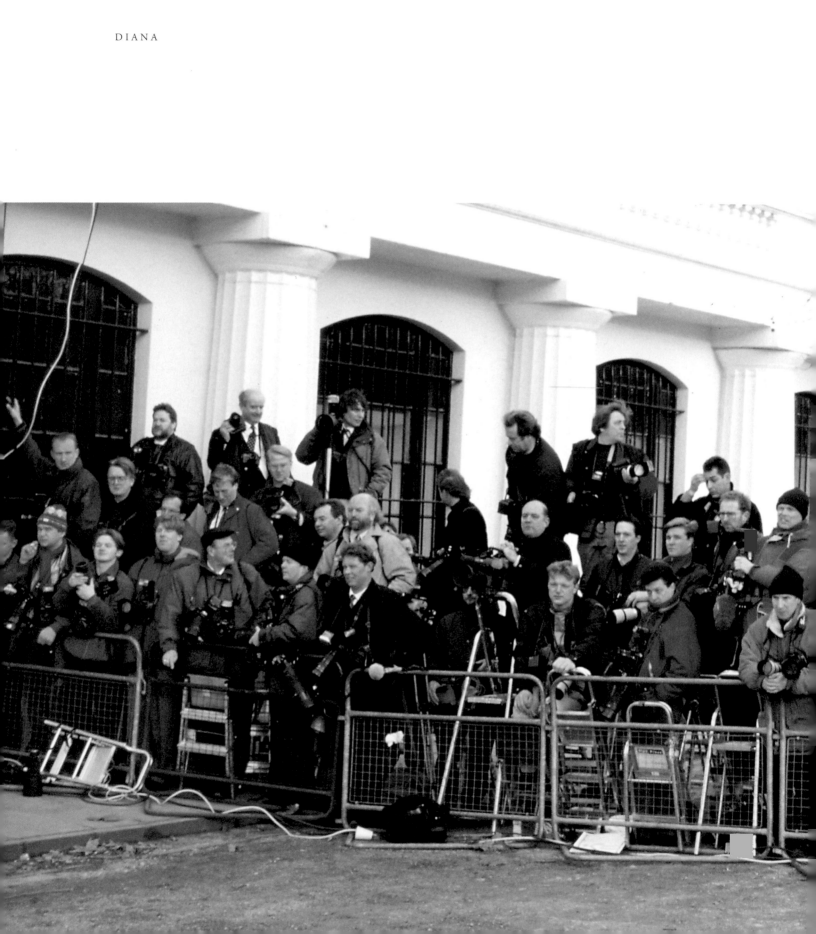

"A girl given the name of the ancient goddess of hunting was, in the end, the most hunted person of the modern age."
— THE EARL SPENCER

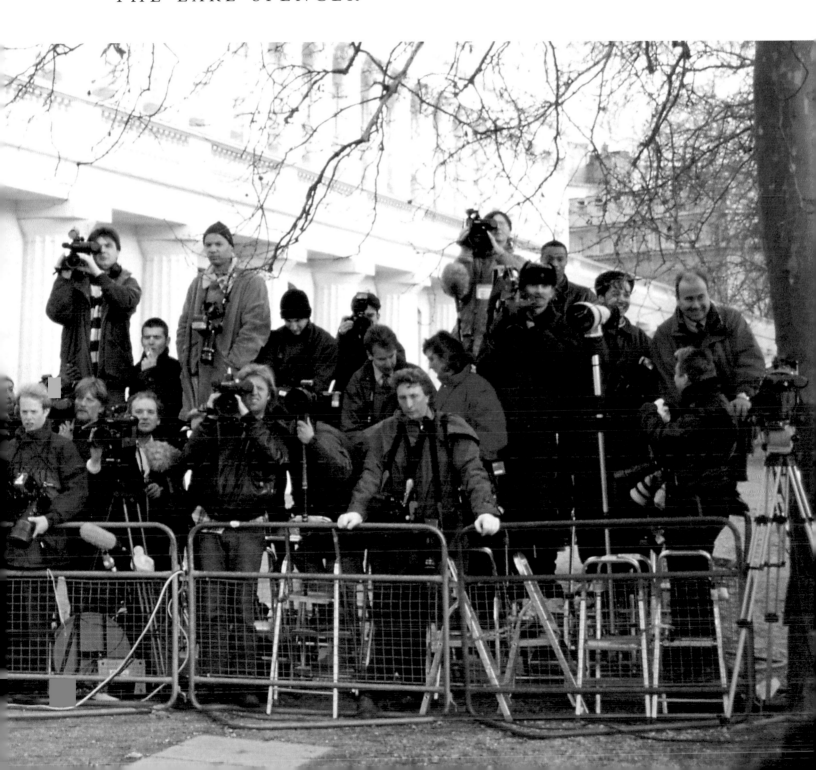

Photography was an essential tool of her public work, beaming out to the world pictures of her walking though a minefield in Angola, embracing lepers in India, visiting cancer hospices wherever she went. She also used them, knowingly, to convey her natural charms, occasionally in contrast with her husband. But pictures of her dancing with Charles in Australia were some of the happiest ever taken of them; Diana dancing at the White House with John Travolta, or on the London stage with Wayne Sleep, are some of her fan club's happiest memories. Again the images crowd back in: Diana holding the hand of the wife of Hungary's new president when nerves had made her burst into tears; grinning coyly amid scantily-clad lifeguards on Bondi Beach, Sydney; sharing her apprehensions with the camera before an exotic Arabian feast; Diana meeting the Pope in Rome or gracing a gondola in Venice, riding a stagecoach in the American west or frolicking with Fergie on the Swiss ski slopes.

Family images helped keep the marital myth going long after it had become a lie. The tabloid sycophancy of the 1980s was bound to turn sour when Diana appeared to be the one rocking the royal boat. But she could never understand the lies they told, simply to sell newspapers. Nor, once she had famously asked for "time and space", could she stomach their relentless focus on her private life. "I can never enjoy any weekend," she once told me, "until I know someone else is on the front page of the *News of the World.*"

As her marriage broke down, she used photographs to convey secret messages to her admirers, like those poignant "postcards home" from the Taj Mahal and the Pyramids – powerful, silent symbols that she felt abandoned, a woman alone. Or that final trip with Charles to Korea, where she grimaced and even he could not hide his unhappiness, to the point where the papers back home dubbed them "The Glums". Photography helped to re-establish herself, after her divorce, as a stylishly independent woman; but it also frustrated her attempts to return to some normalcy, as when she was captured unawares by a hidden camera in her London gym, even caught with a new beau by the closed-circuit cameras in one of her favourite Knightsbridge stores.

The last years of her life were haunted by those leather-clad men on motorbikes, cameras at the ready, who lurked at her gates and followed her everywhere, night and day, in the hope of a single picture that could literally make them millions. Once she had left the royal family, she believed herself – logically but hopelessly – to have become a private citizen again, happy to work with the media when about her public duties, but entitled to be left alone when off duty, in private. It was a poignant misconception she could not be talked out of.

"Those who live by the media die by the media," as one callous critic put it, little realising his pat platitude might turn out to contain a chilling germ of truth. Yes, Diana was to some extent a creation of the media, whom she knowingly used to shape her own image and advance the causes close to her heart; but no, she did not deserve to become their victim, hunted and hounded, perhaps literally, to death.

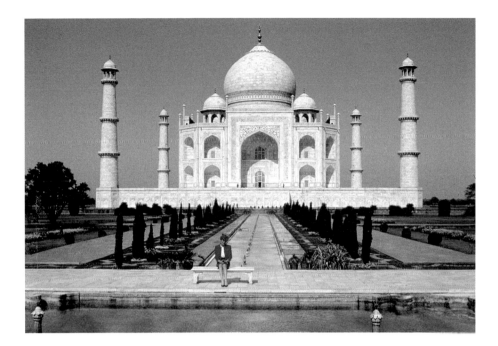

Left, a "postcard home" from the Taj Mahal, India, 1992.

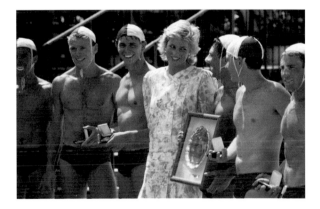

Above, Bondi Beach, Australia, 1988.

Right, Venice, 1985.

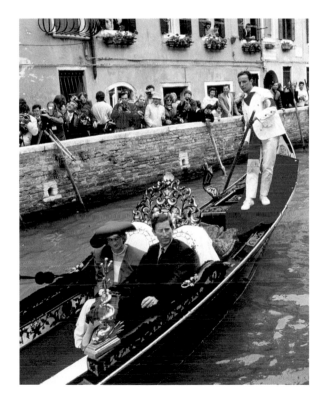

DANCE

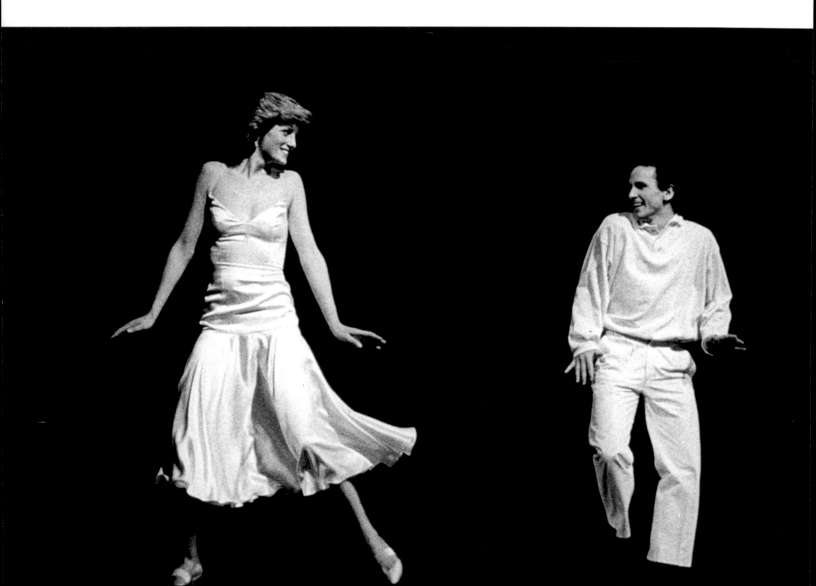

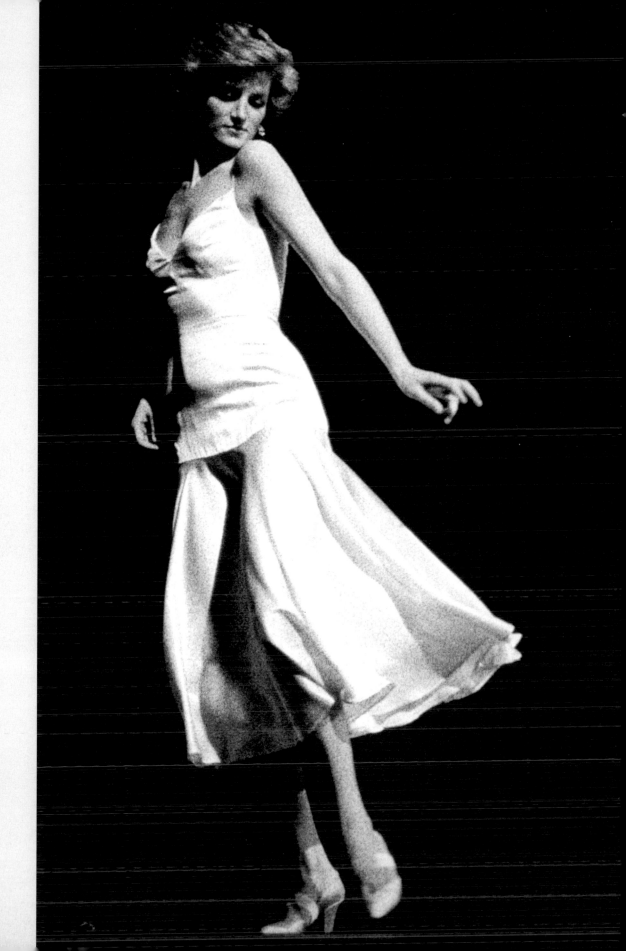

Dancing with
Wayne Sleep,
1985.

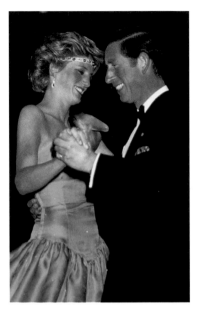
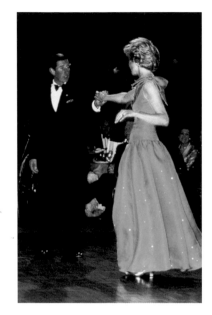

Pictures of her dancing with Charles in
Australia were some of the happiest
ever taken of them. Diana dancing at
the White House with John Travolta,
or on the London stage with Wayne
Sleep, are some of her fan club's
happiest memories.

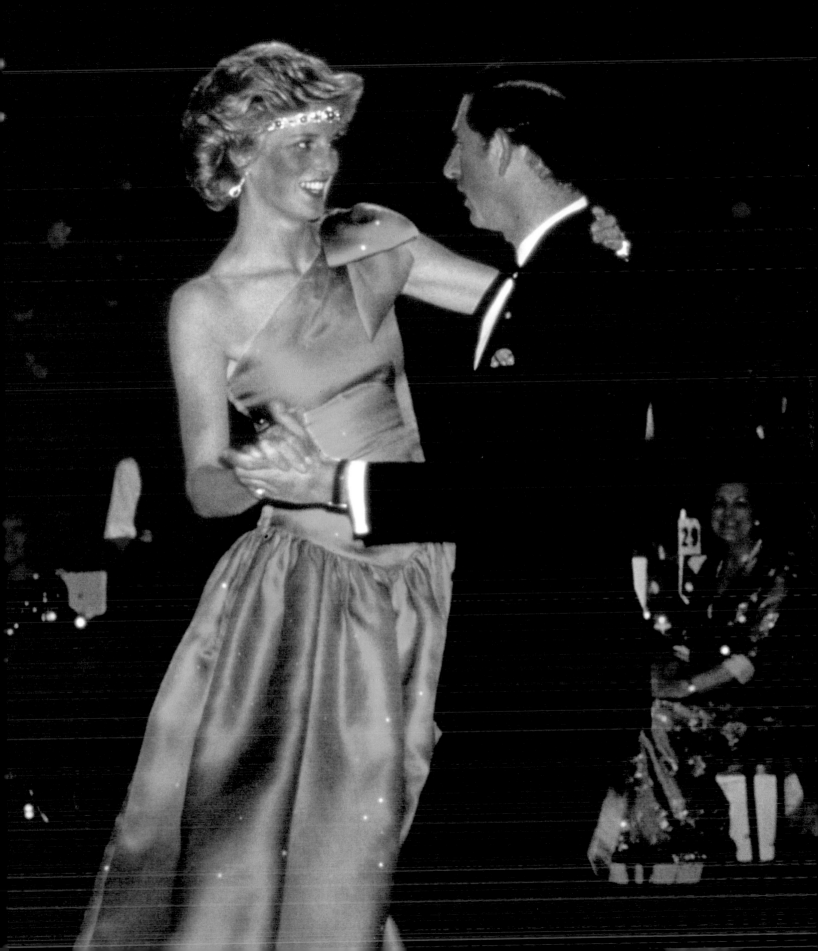

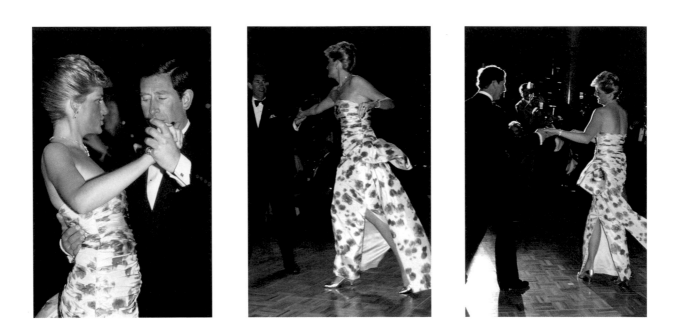

"The world has lost a vibrant,
lovely young person."
– THE ARCHBISHOP OF CANTERBURY

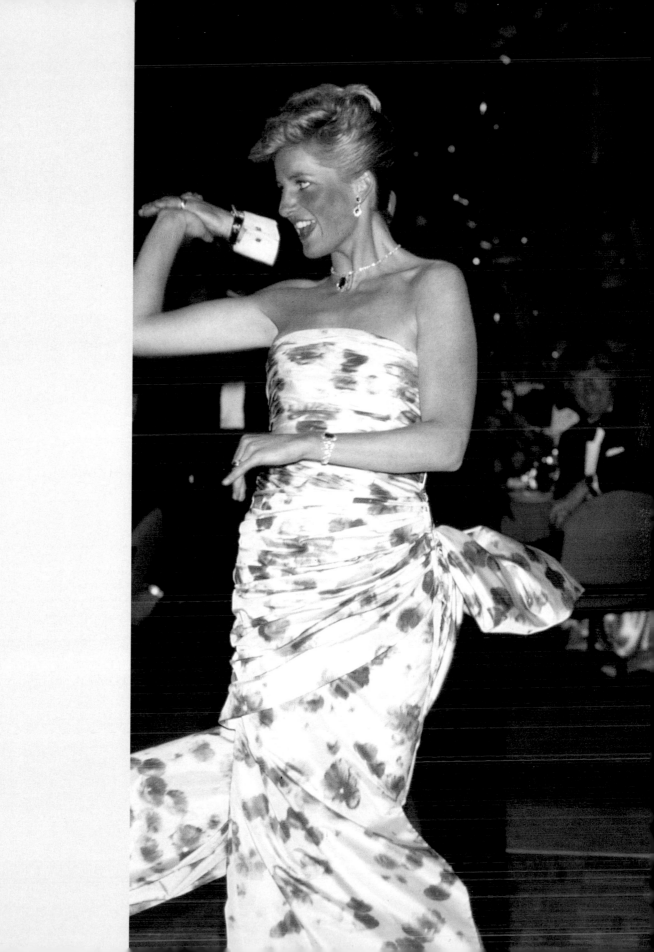

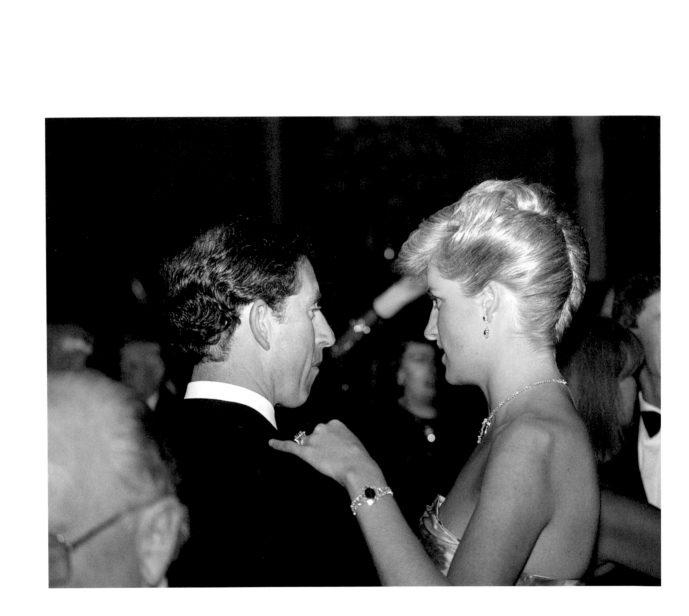

Above, dancing with
Prince Charles in
Australia in 1988; and
(*opposite*) with John
Travolta at the White
House in 1985.

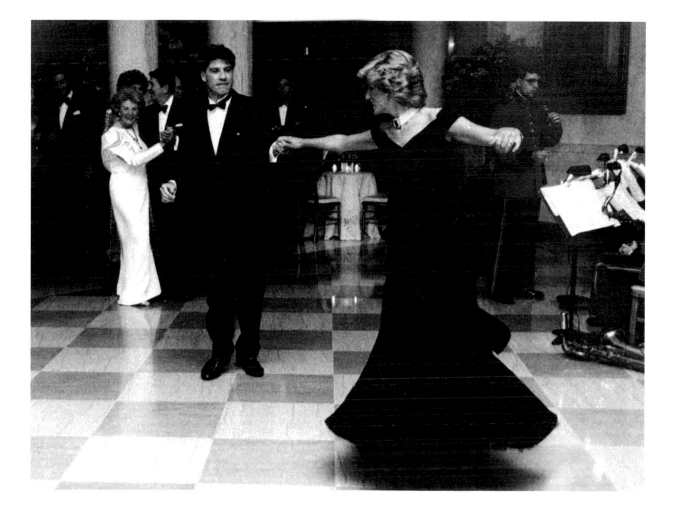

Some photographs were more "official" than others. Of the unauthorised pictures inevitably taken of her, wherever she went, there were many which captured her private self charmingly enough to win her eventual approval.

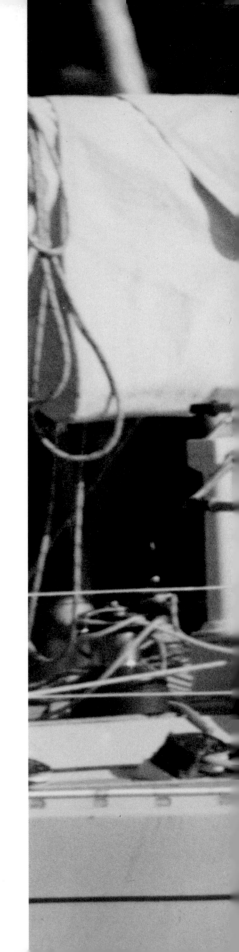

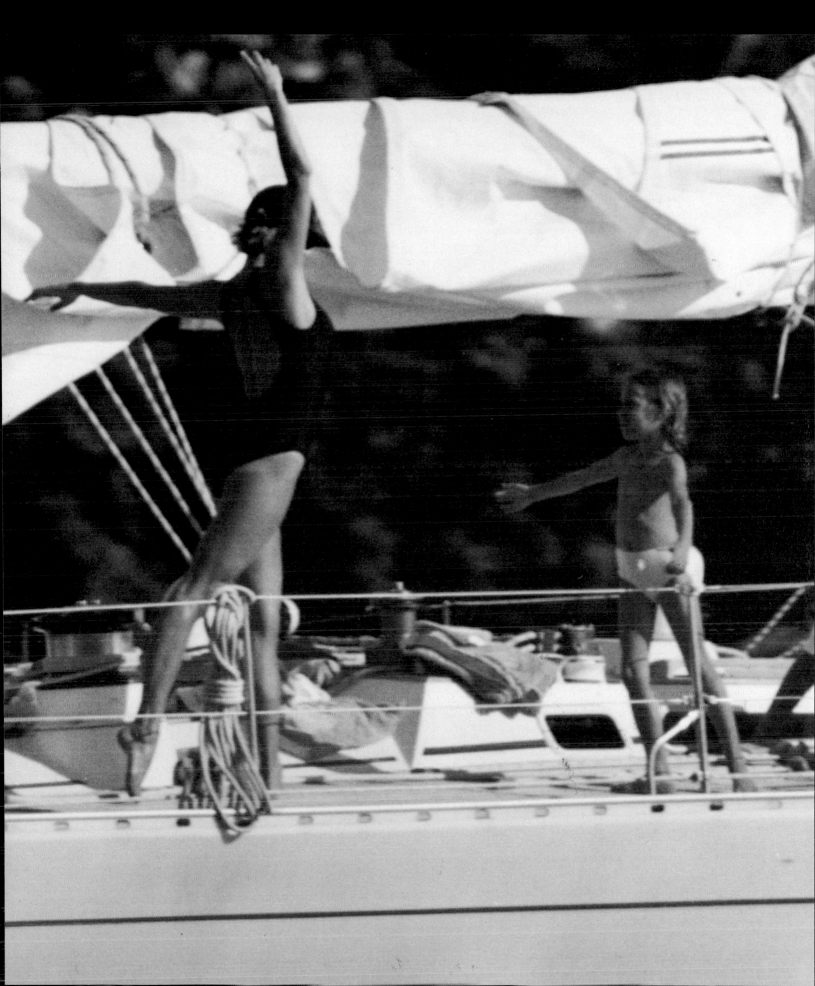

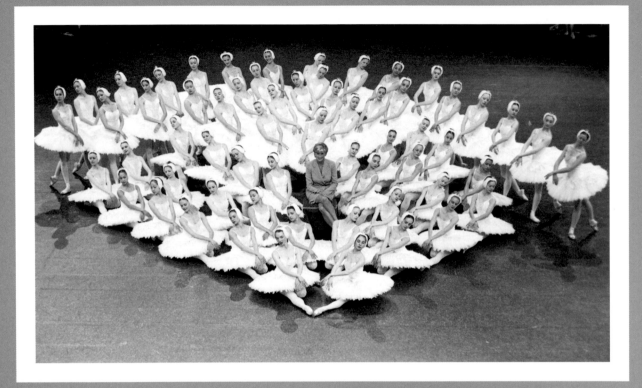

The English National Ballet, 1997.

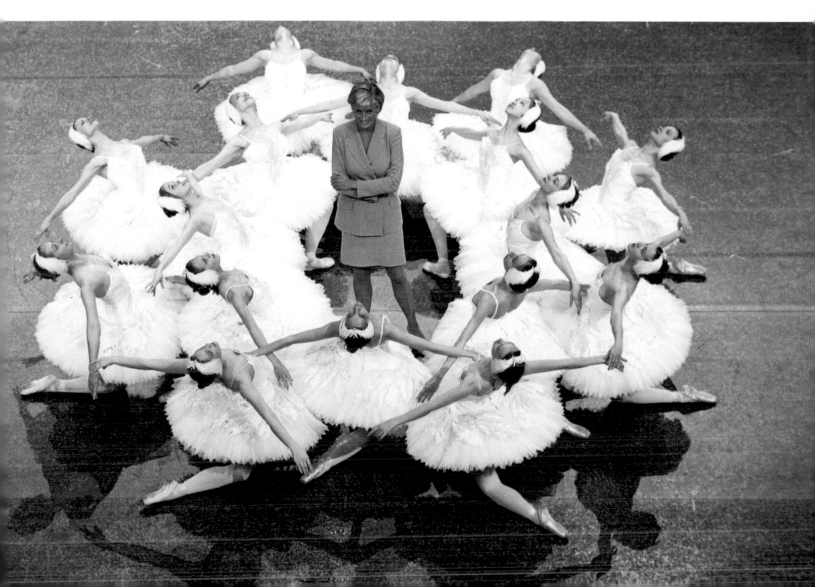

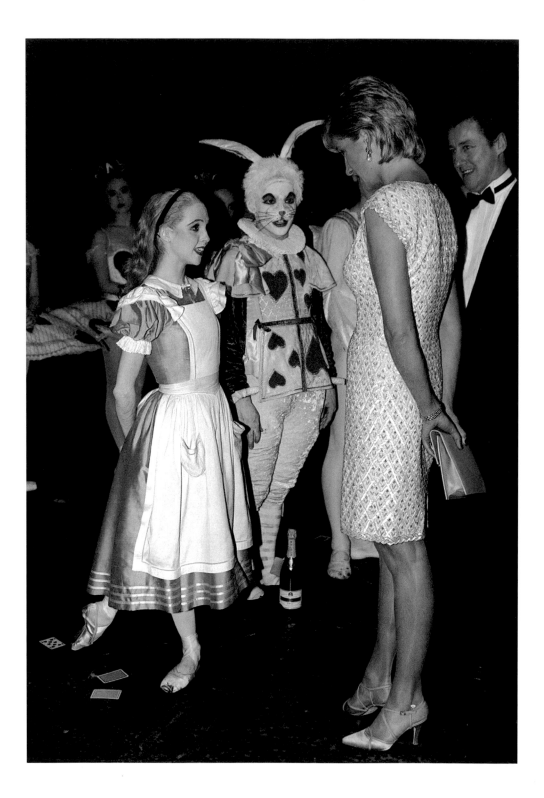

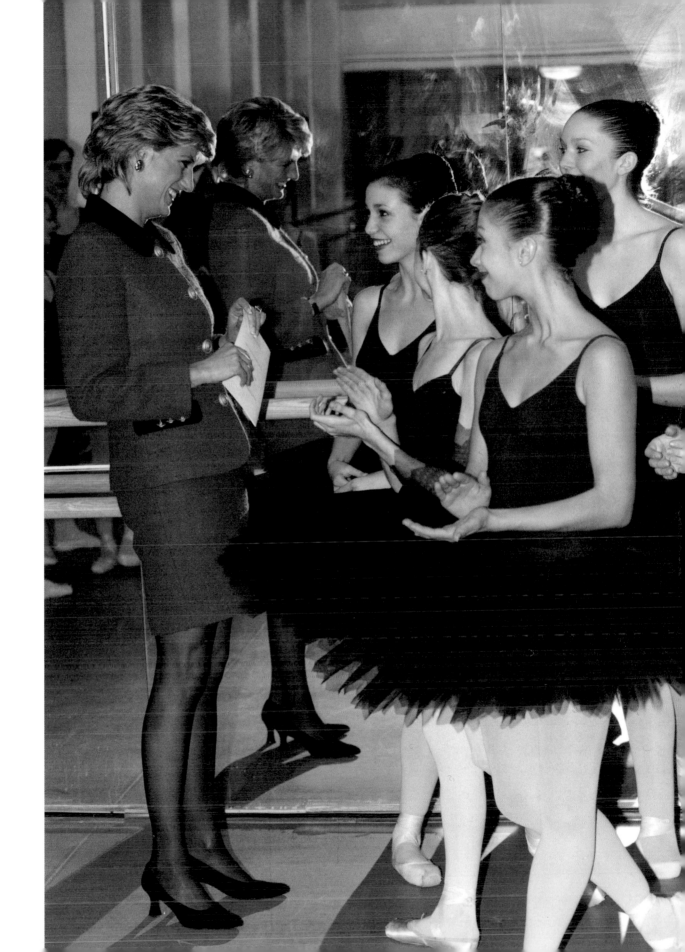

LIMELIGHT

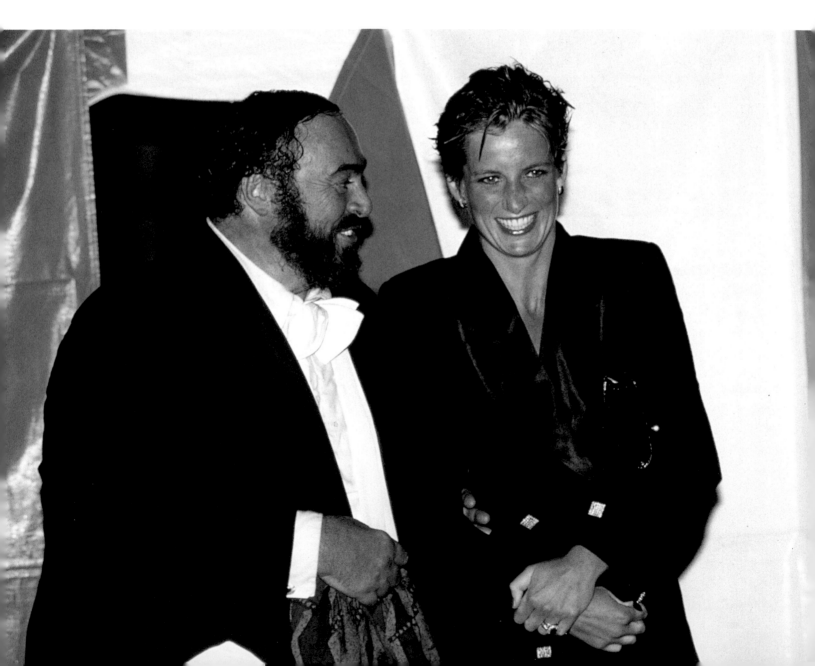

"My heart is full of grief and pain. She was the most beautiful symbol of humanity and love for all the world."
— LUCIANO PAVAROTTI

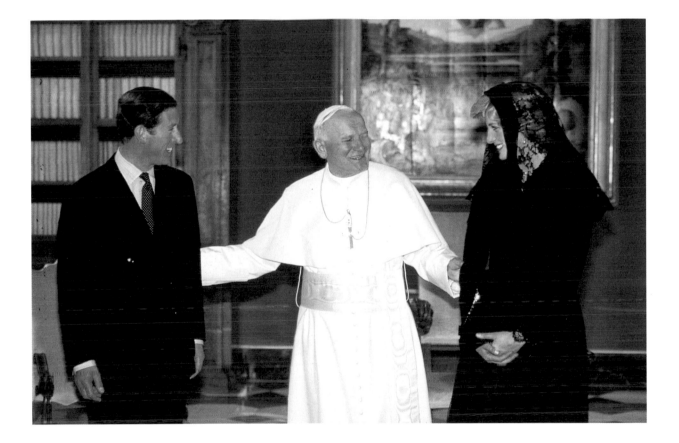

Left, with Luciano Pavarotti in the rain, Hyde Park, London, 1991.

Above, the Pope, 1985. *Overleaf*, Princess Grace of Monaco, 1981.

Pages 124-25, with the King and Queen of Spain.

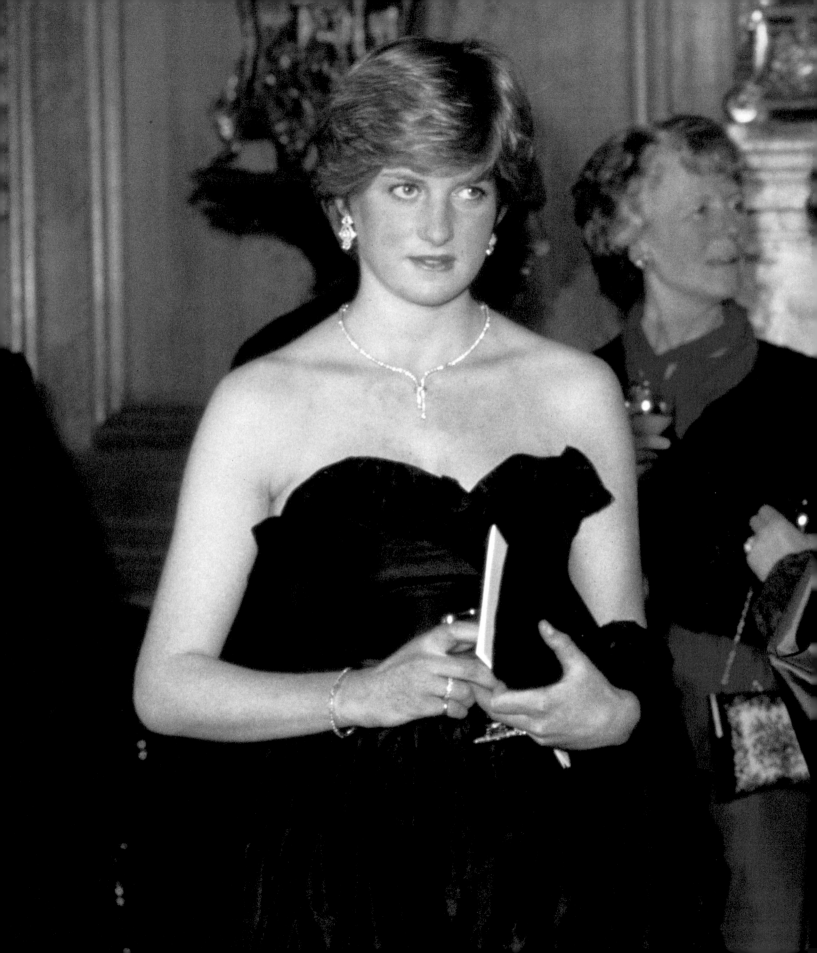

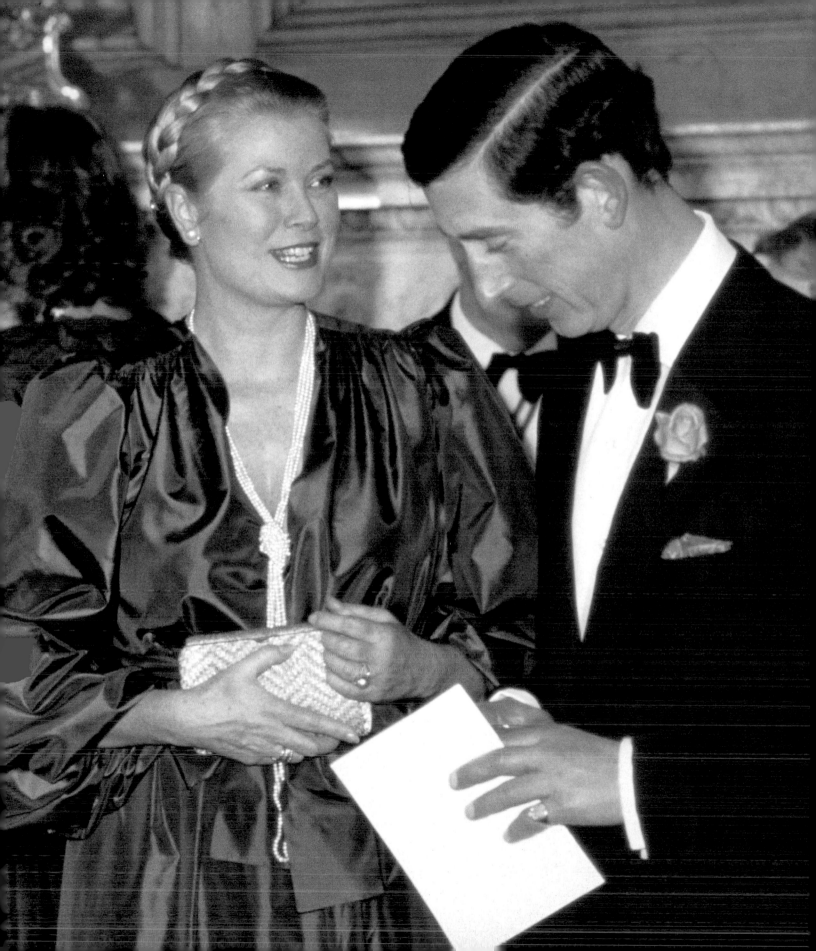

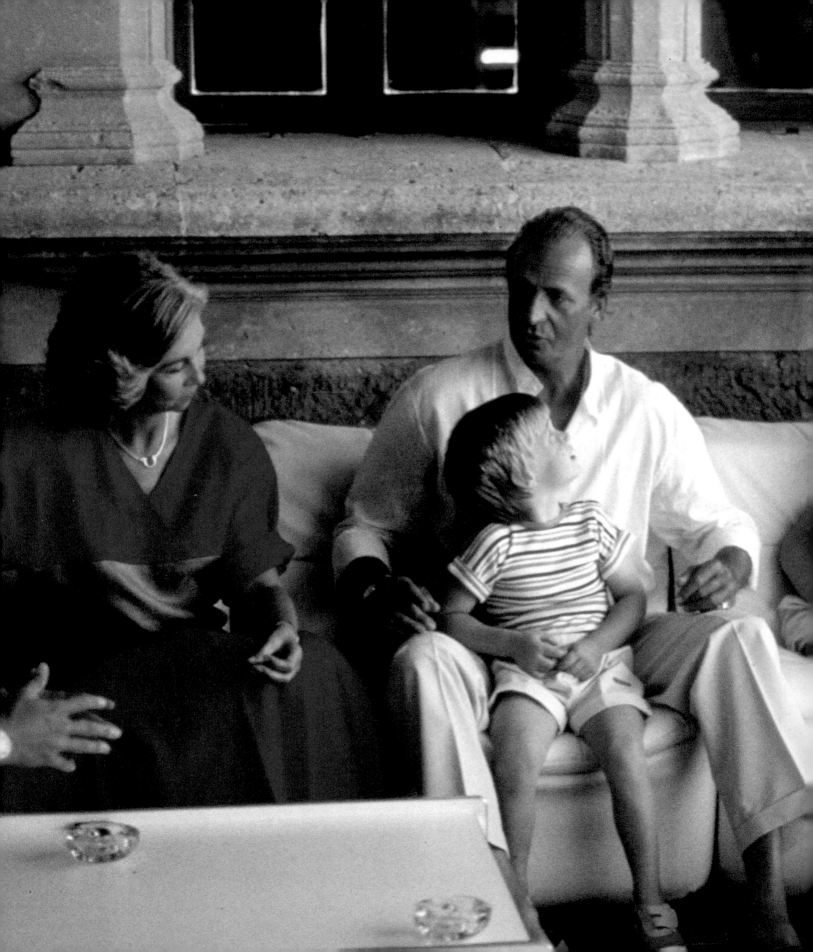

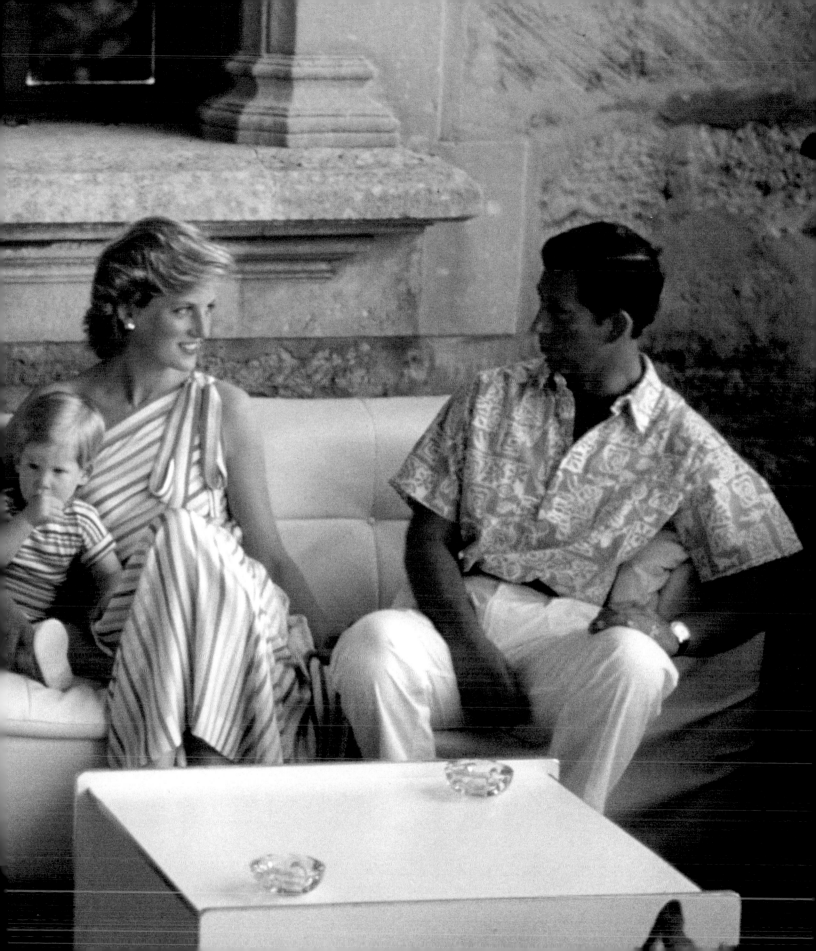

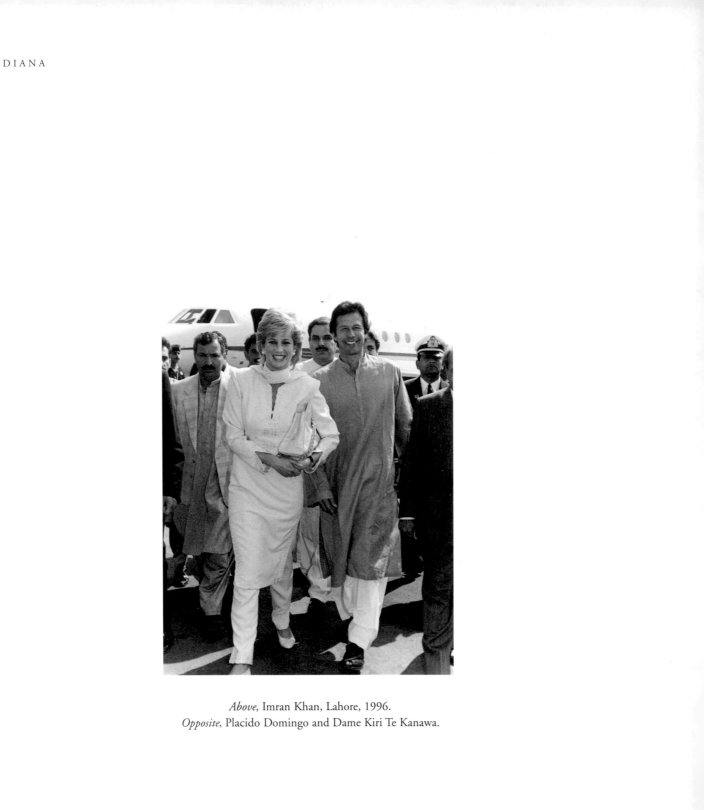

Above, Imran Khan, Lahore, 1996.
Opposite, Placido Domingo and Dame Kiri Te Kanawa.

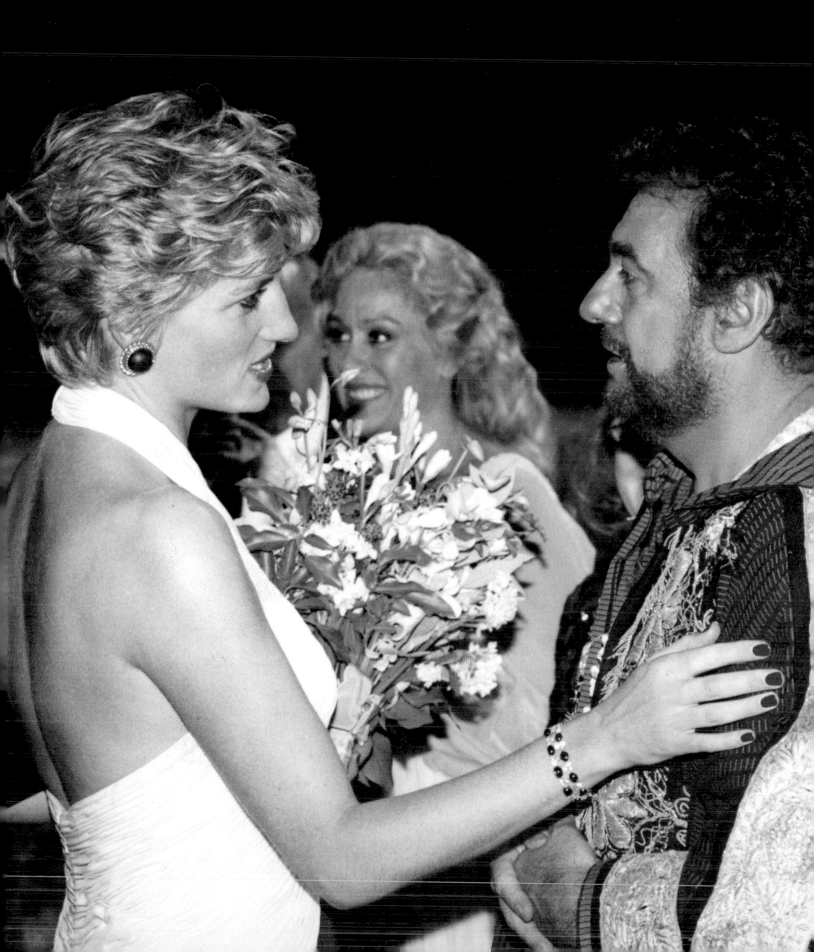

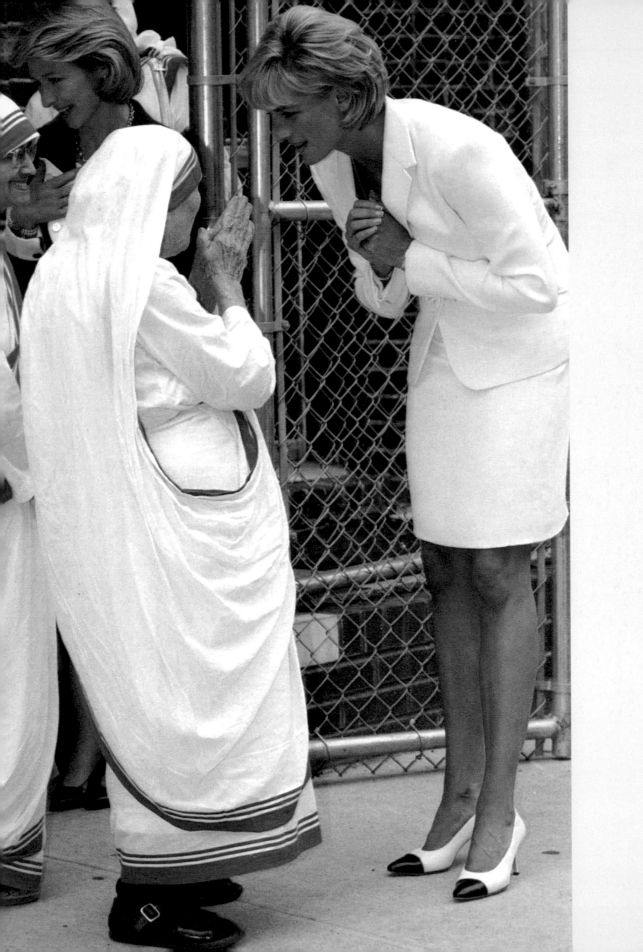

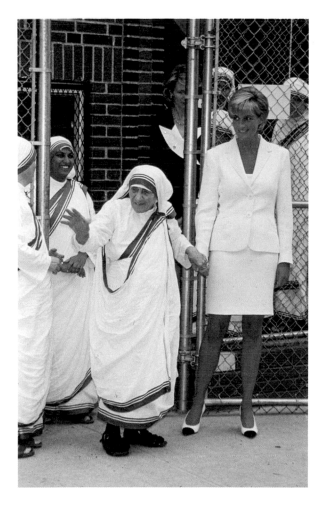

"To heal other people, you
have to suffer yourself."
— MOTHER TERESA

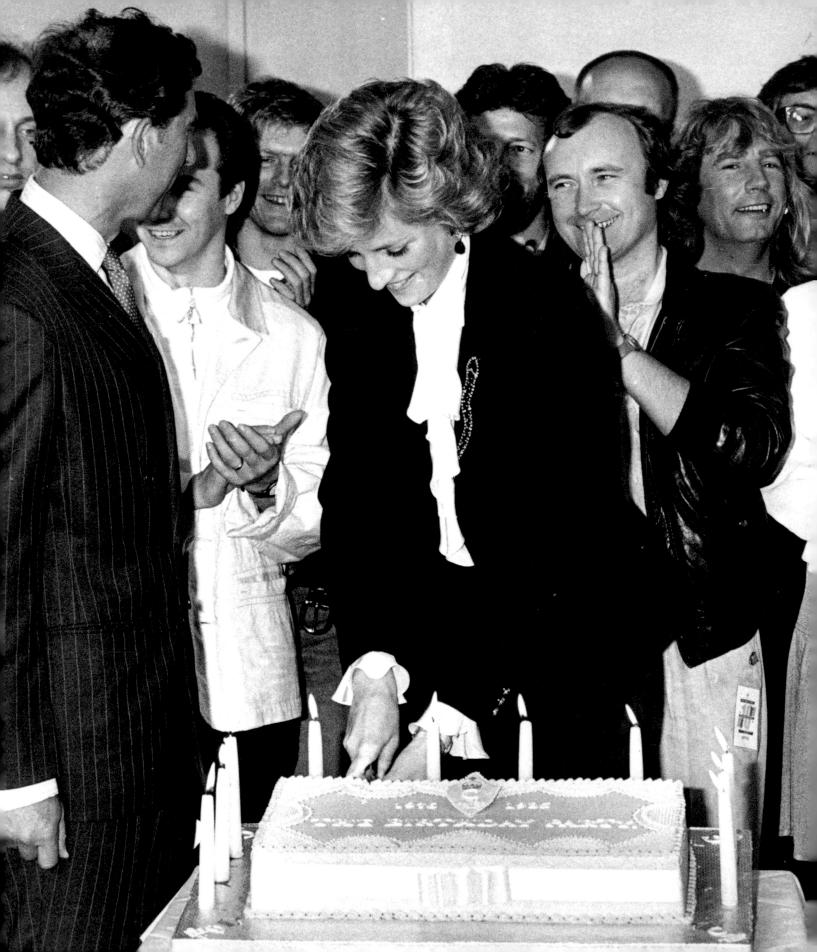

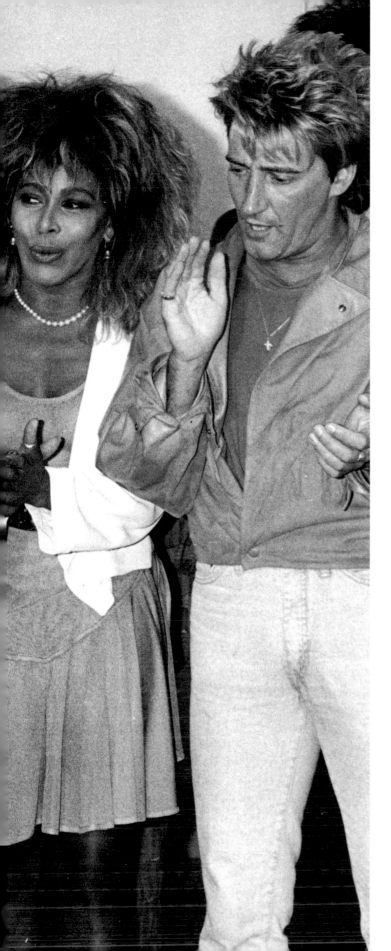

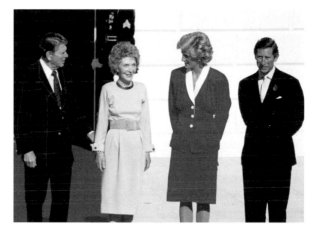

Above, President and Mrs Ronald Reagan, 1985.

Left, a charity rock concert, Wembley, 1986.

"I truly believe that some souls are too special, too beautiful, to be kept from heaven, however painful it is for the rest of us to let them go.... God bless you, Diana, you will surely rest in peace."
— GEORGE MICHAEL

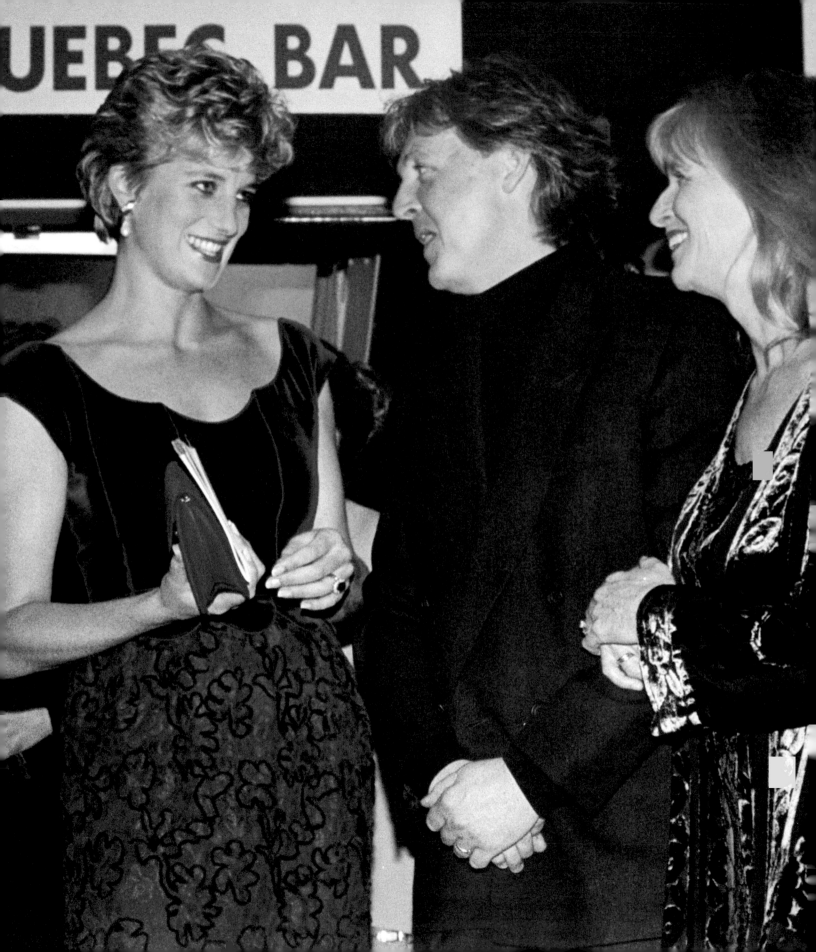

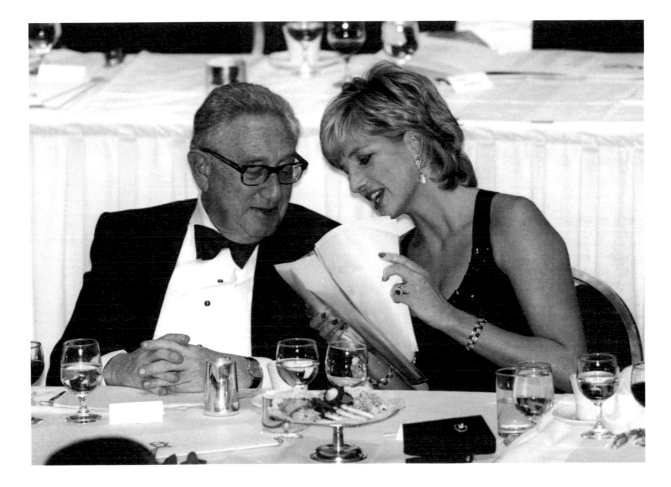

Above, with Henry Kissinger at the Humanitarian of the Year award ceremony, New York, 1992.

Opposite, Paul and Linda McCartney, 1992.

"I knew her as a very sensitive, at times very amusing, lady who desperately wanted to make a difference to the world."
— HENRY KISSINGER

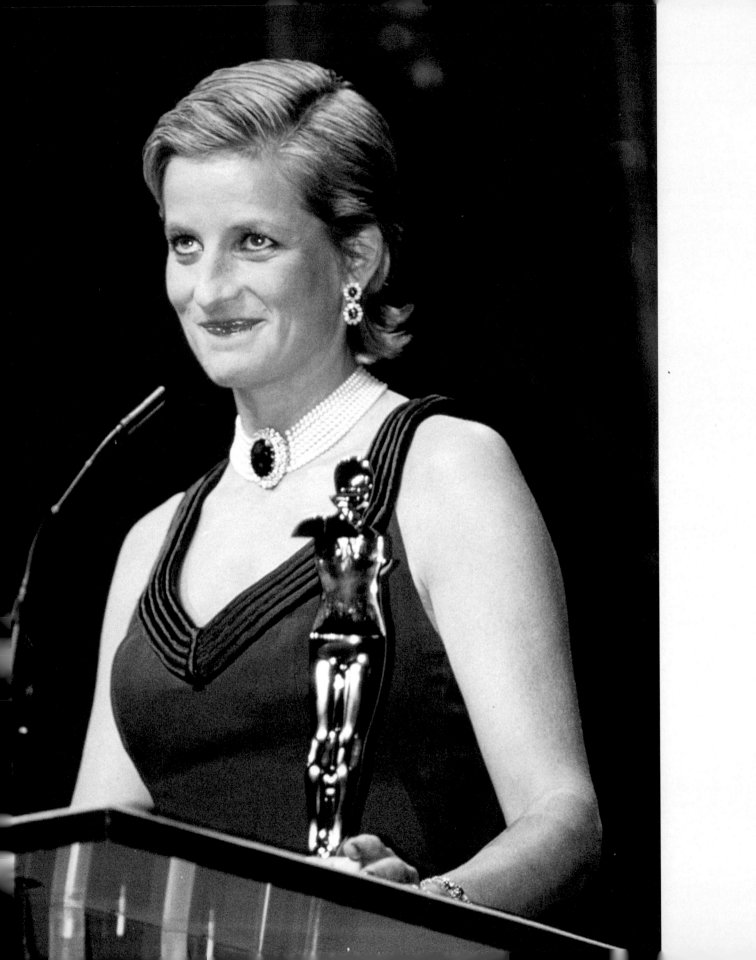

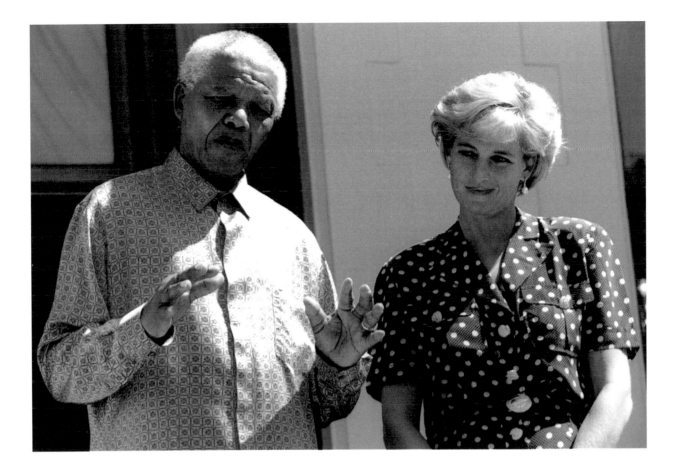

Above, Nelson Mandela, Cape Town, 1997.

Opposite, the Council of Fashion Designers of America awards, New York, 1995.

"She was an ambassador for victims of landmines, war orphans, the sick and needy throughout the world. She was undoubtedly one of the best ambassadors of Great Britain."

— NELSON MANDELA

CAMPAIGNS

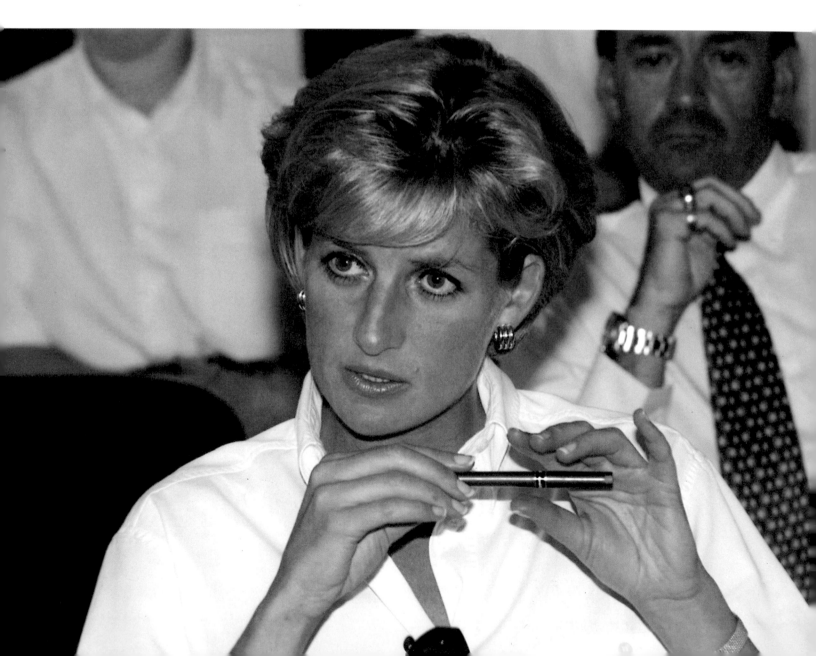

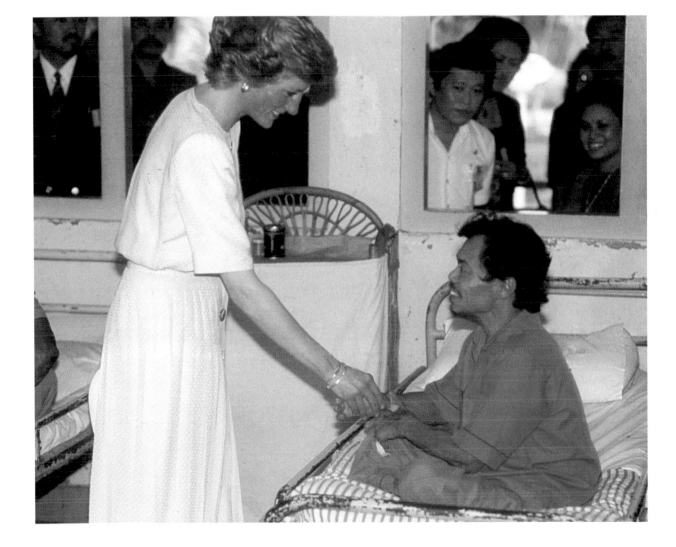

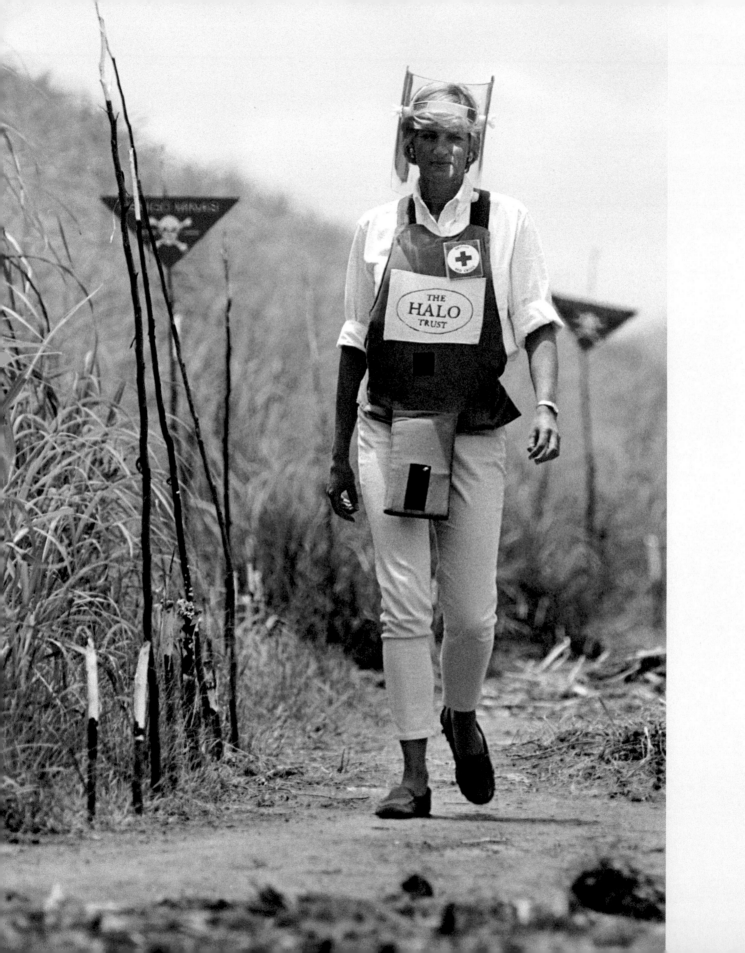

In the last nine months of her life, via trips to Angola and Bosnia, she altered government policy on landmines on both sides of the Atlantic.

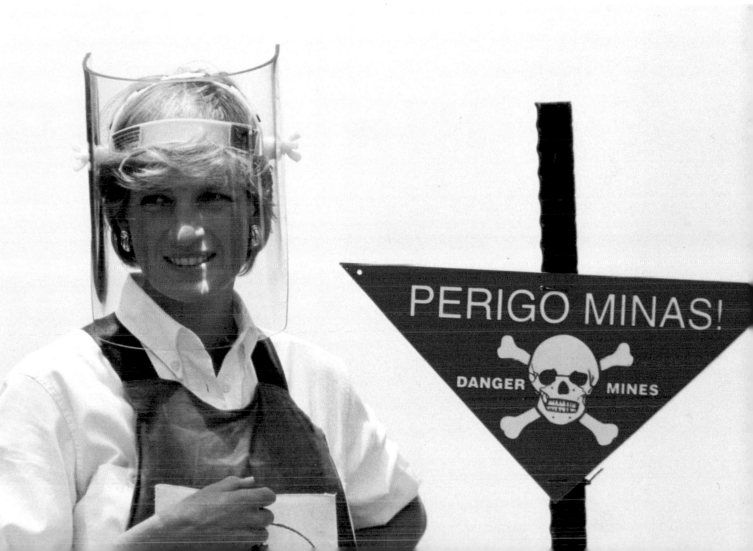

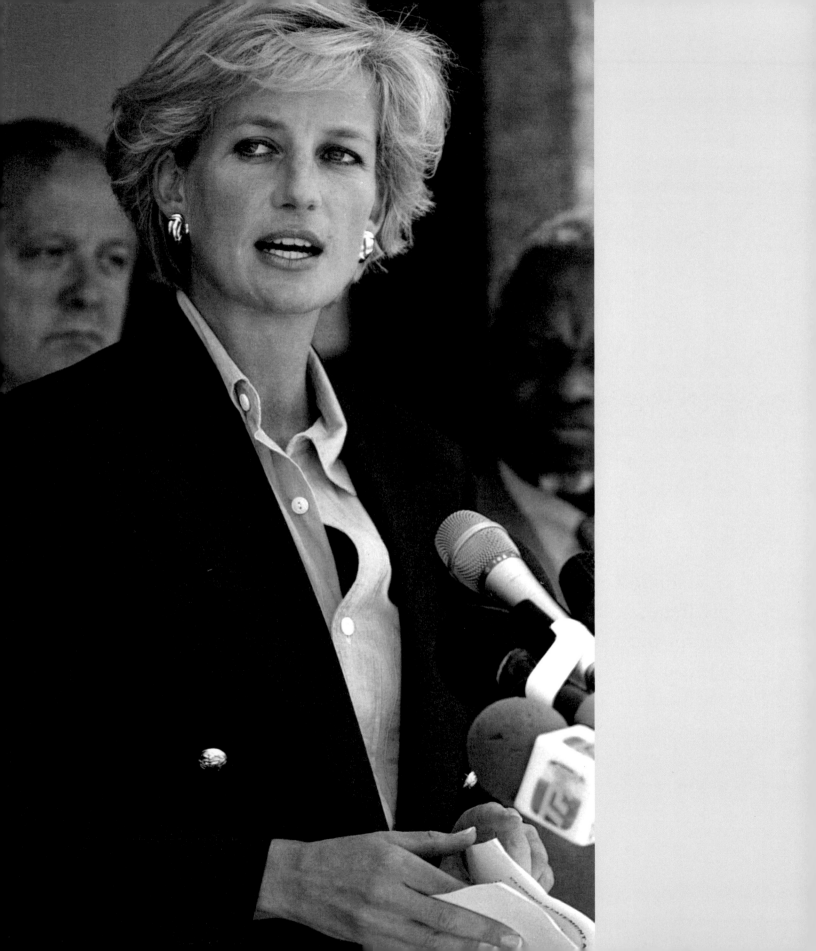

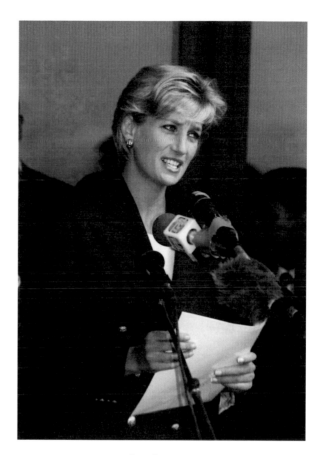

Angola, 1997.

"We admired her work for children, for people with AIDS and for the discouragement of landmines.... I will always be glad I knew the Princess... all of us have lost a friend and a strong voice for those less fortunate."

— BILL CLINTON

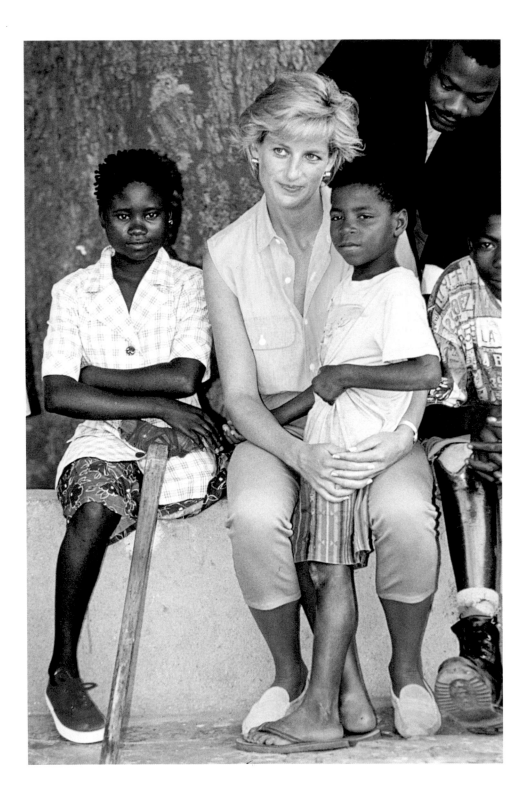

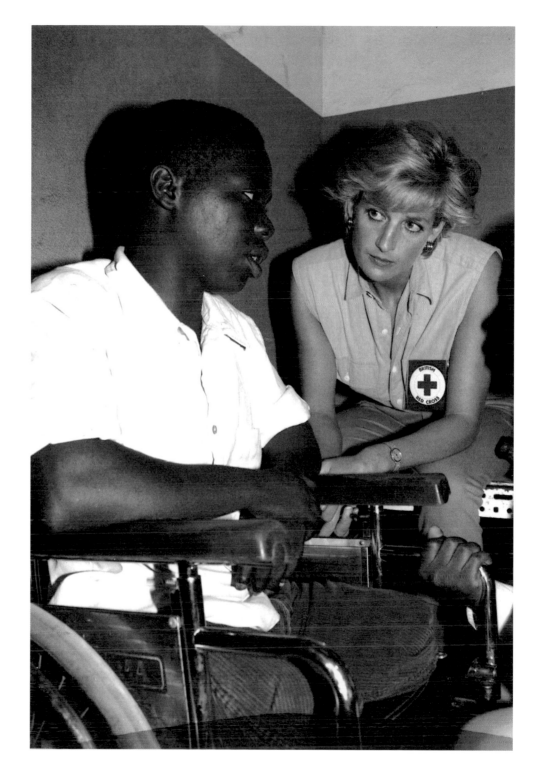

Angola, 1997.

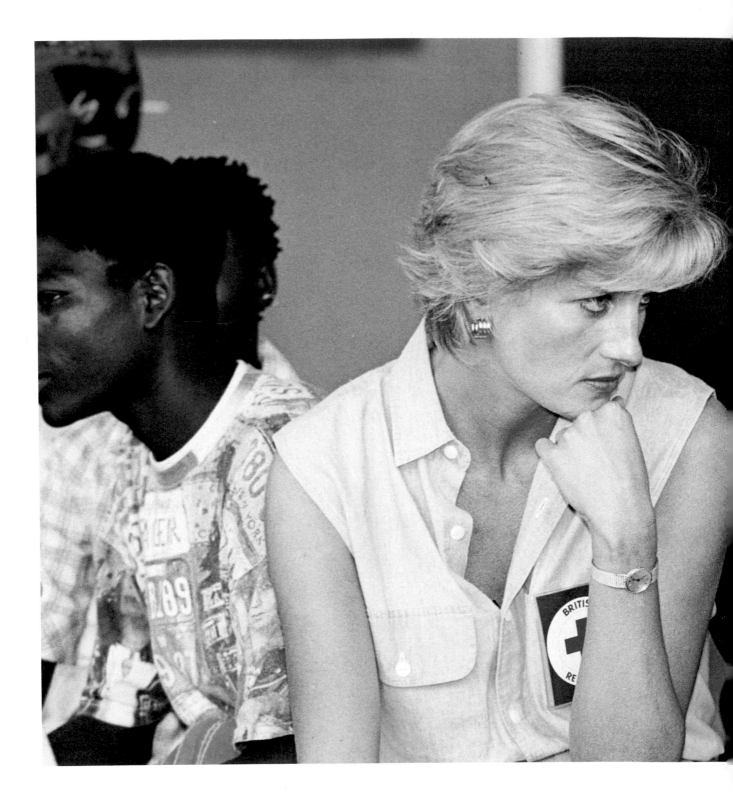

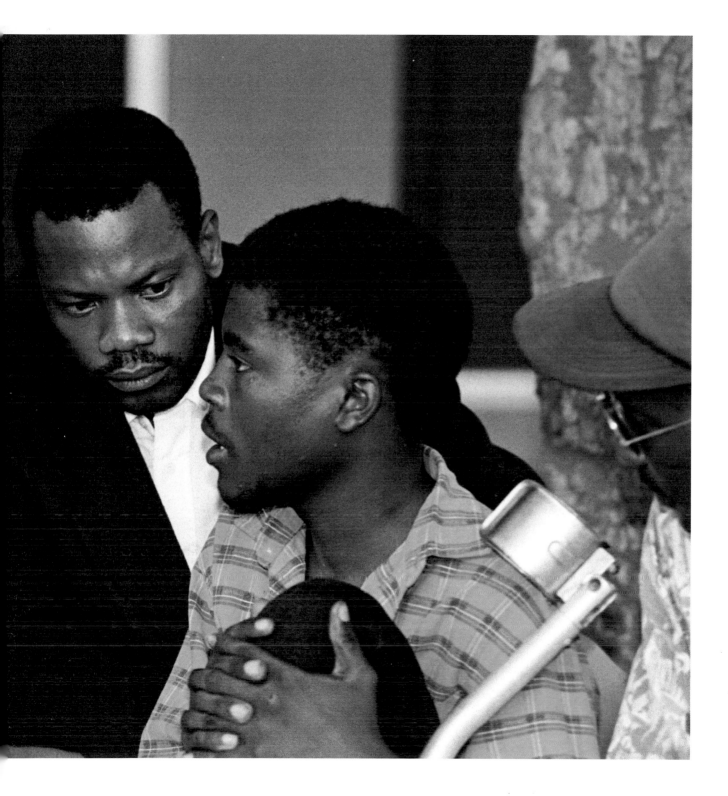

Now we have time to reflect, irresistibly wondering what might have been, an insupportable poignancy comes to surround every stage of Diana's all too brief life. If only her mother had not felt compelled to leave... if only Charles had married Camilla in the first place... if only he had been capable of understanding the deceptively complex woman he married instead... if only Diana had been a few years older when she fell in love with him... if only he had known what love meant... if only they had stayed together, for the sake of their children if not the nation... if only she and Dodi had not gone to Paris that day, not got into that car....

If only, if only. One of the most potent came from Diana herself, barely two months before she died, at a private lunch in New York with two expatriate British women, both high media flyers. Asked by Tina Brown, editor of *The New Yorker*, if she regretted the loss of her chance to become Queen, Diana unhesitatingly muttered "Yes, yes," her eyes modestly lowered. Then she raised them to proclaim: "We would have been the best team in the world. I could shake hands till the cows come home. And Charles could make serious speeches. But..." – she shook her head sadly – "it was not to be."

So many things were not to be. A life abroad, perhaps, as she admitted contemplating in the last interview she gave, ironically to a French newspaper. "If it were not for my boys," she told *Le Monde*, "I would have left Britain years ago." She especially favoured America – "the optimism, the options, the openness", as it seemed to Tina Brown, whom she told she would "love to move here". On a fund-raising visit to Chicago the previous year, she told me, the crush of the crowds had been "really scary." But it would not stop her going there, as often as she could, perhaps even buying a Manhattan *pied-à-terre*. From there, after all, it was the merest hop to her favourite Caribbean hideaways, Richard Branson's Necker Island, in the British Virgins, or the K Club in Barbuda.

Spending time abroad, both private and public, was important to Diana in her sustained attempts to become an unofficial international ambassador for Britain – a role denied her under the Conservative government, but formally endorsed by Tony Blair just days before her death. With his own instinctive feel for the "presentational" side of public issues, he knew that Diana needed only some government support and infrastructure to win millions in exports for Britain, and help his own mission to modernise the country's creaking image around the world. For her part, Diana savoured her new role as a force for good on the international stage, but she never forgot her roots, and wanted to do something for Britain. She had, after all, proved she could do it.

Once an ex-royal, but determined to continue a public role, she did not hesitate to take her campaigns for urgent, contemporary causes to the farthest corners of the world, transcending the mundane political frontiers which tend to hold others back. Her work for cancer hospitals and charities took her on high-profile fund-raising visits to America, Australia, Russia as much as unpublicised visits, often during lonely weekends in London without the children, to people dying in hospices. In the last nine months of her own life, via trips to Angola and Bosnia, she altered government policy on landmines on both sides of the Atlantic, and had high hopes of seeing a worldwide ban signed at an international conference in the autumn of her death. The British Conservative politicians who complained about her "meddling" made interfering fools of themselves, showing why they had been swept from power. With her cannier instinct for the art of the possible, Diana had transformed the global menace of landmines from a political issue into a humanitarian one. Thanks to her it became, to all but a few rent-a-quote backbenchers in search of the oxygen of publicity, entirely above dispute. She had a way of neutralising petty squabbles about matters of life and death.

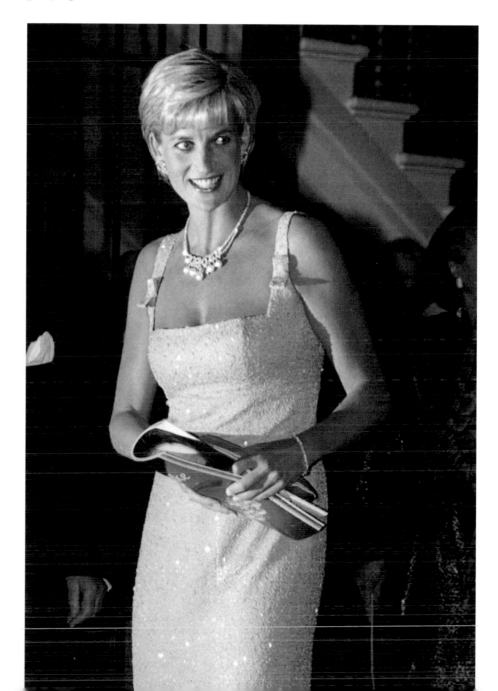

At the Royal Albert Hall,
London, 1997.

FAREWELL

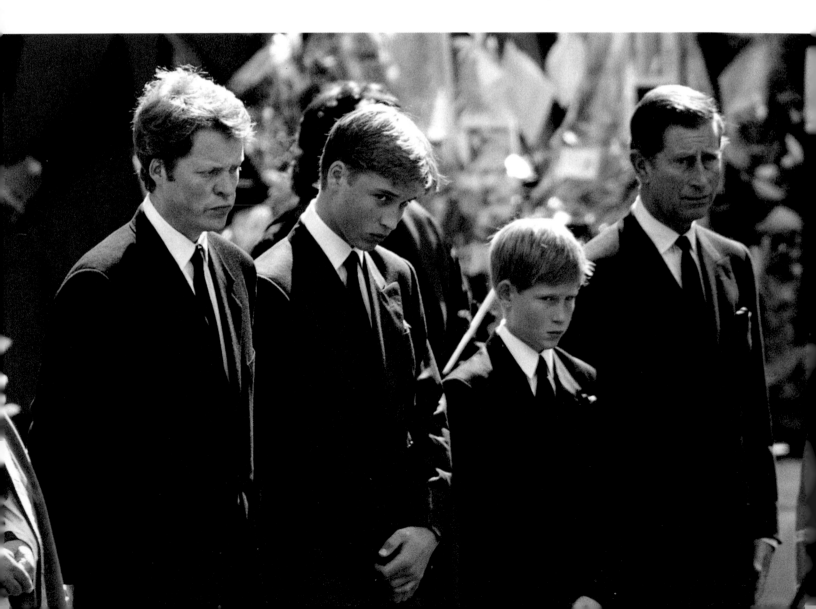

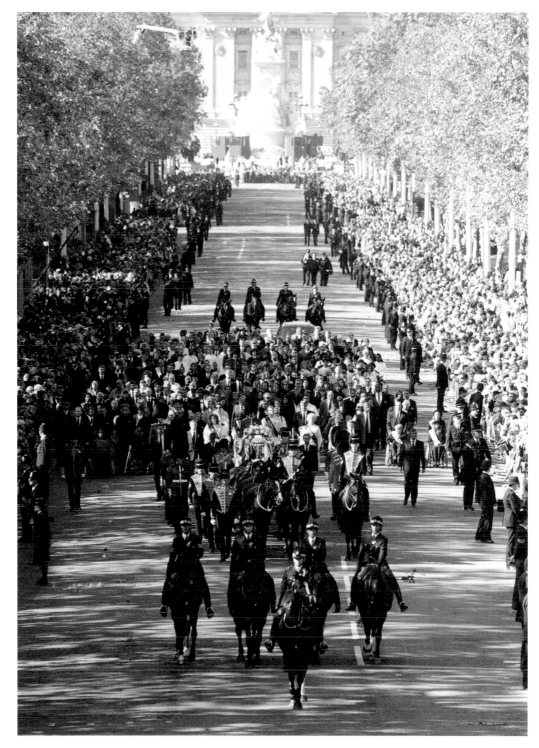

Left, the princes
and Earl Spencer
watch the coffin
loaded into the
hearse.

Right, the cortège
in the Mall,
followed
by charity
representatives.

149

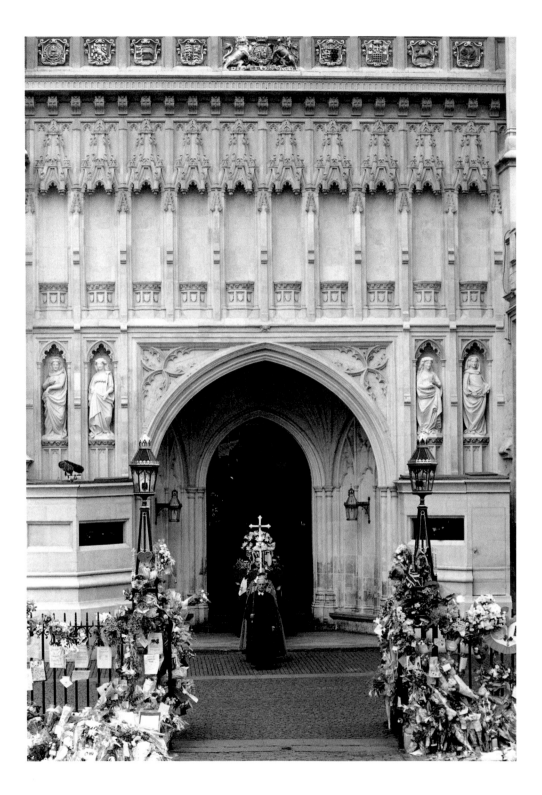

If I should die and leave you here awhile,
Be not like others, sore undone, who keep
Long vigils by the silent dust, and weep.
For my sake – turn again to life and smile,
Nerving thy heart and trembling hand to do
Something to comfort other hearts than thine.
Complete those dear unfinished tasks of mine
And I, perchance, may therein comfort you.

READ BY LADY SARAH McCORQUODALE

Time is too slow for those who wait,
too swift for those who fear,
too long for those who grieve,
too short for those who rejoice,
but for those who love, time is eternity.

READ BY LADY JANE FELLOWES

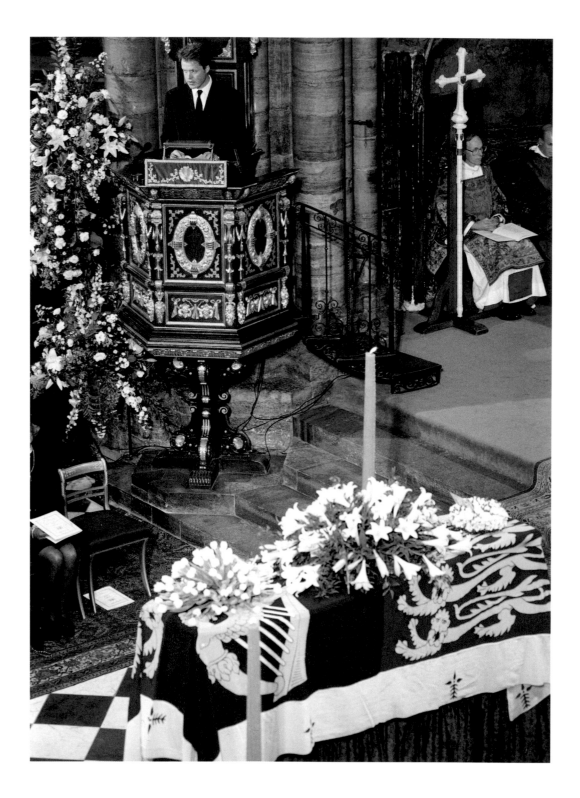

"We give thanks for the life of a woman I am so proud to be able to call my sister, the unique, the complex, the extraordinary and irreplaceable Diana, whose beauty – both internal and external – will never be extinguished from our minds."

– THE EARL SPENCER

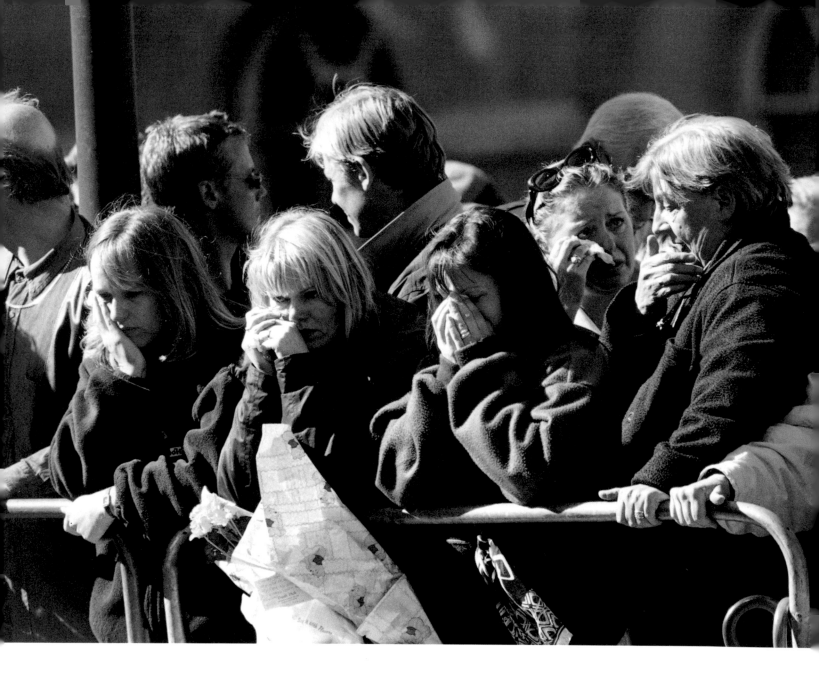

Opposite, outside the gates of Buckingham Palace.

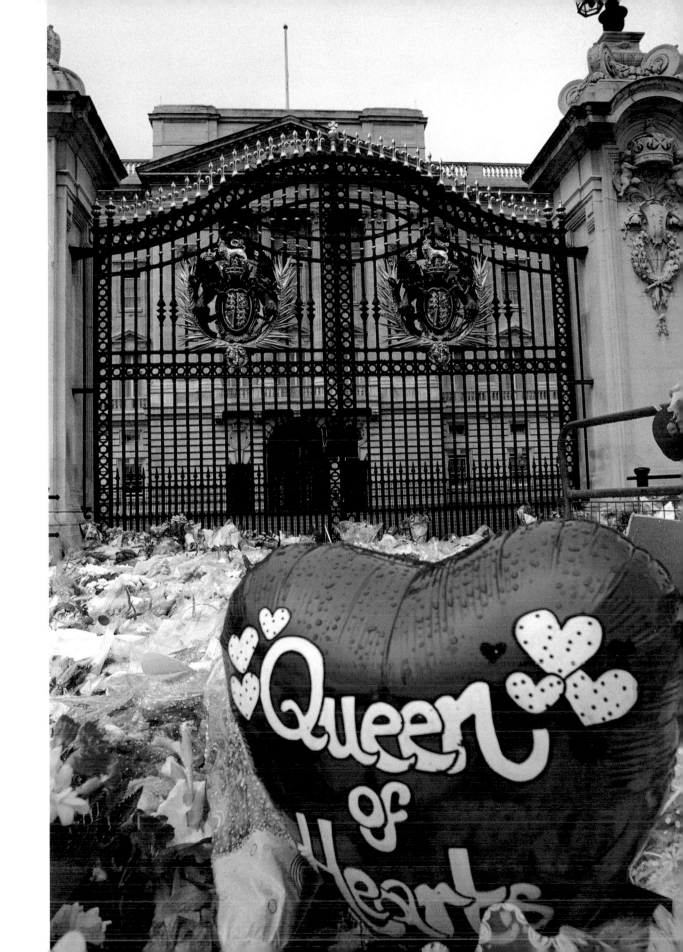

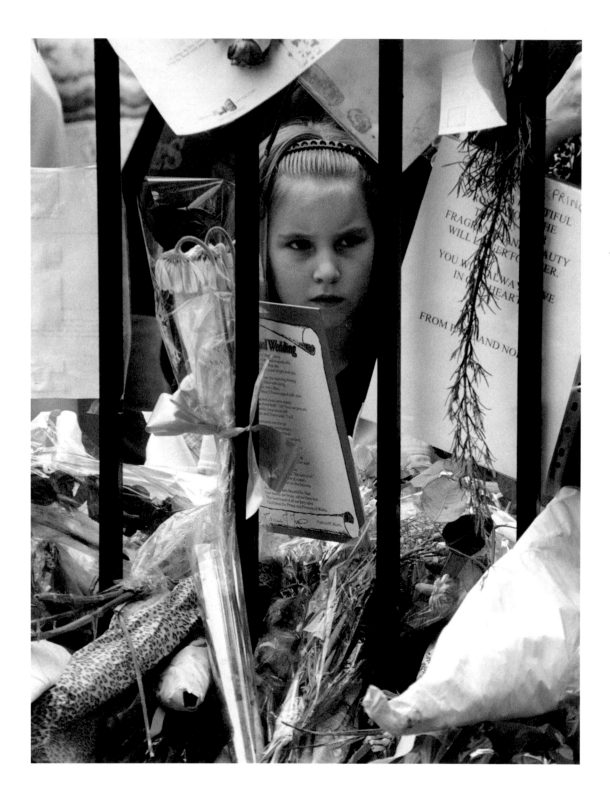

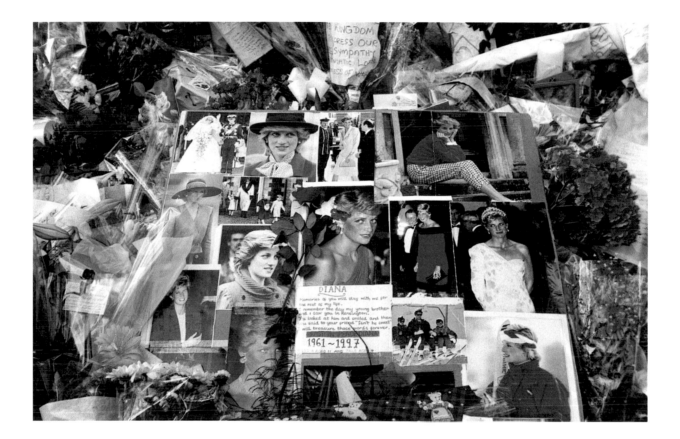

"The world has lost one of its most
compassionate humanitarians, and
I have lost a special friend."
— ELTON JOHN

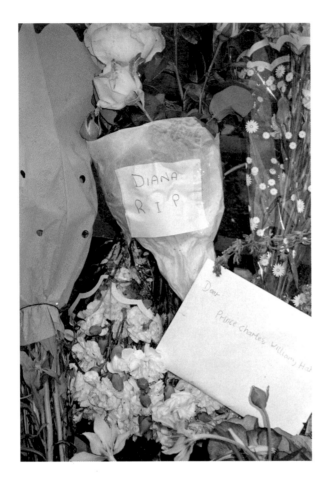

"I want to say how particularly moved and enormously comforted my children and I were, and indeed still are, by the public response to Diana's death."

— H.R.H. THE PRINCE OF WALES

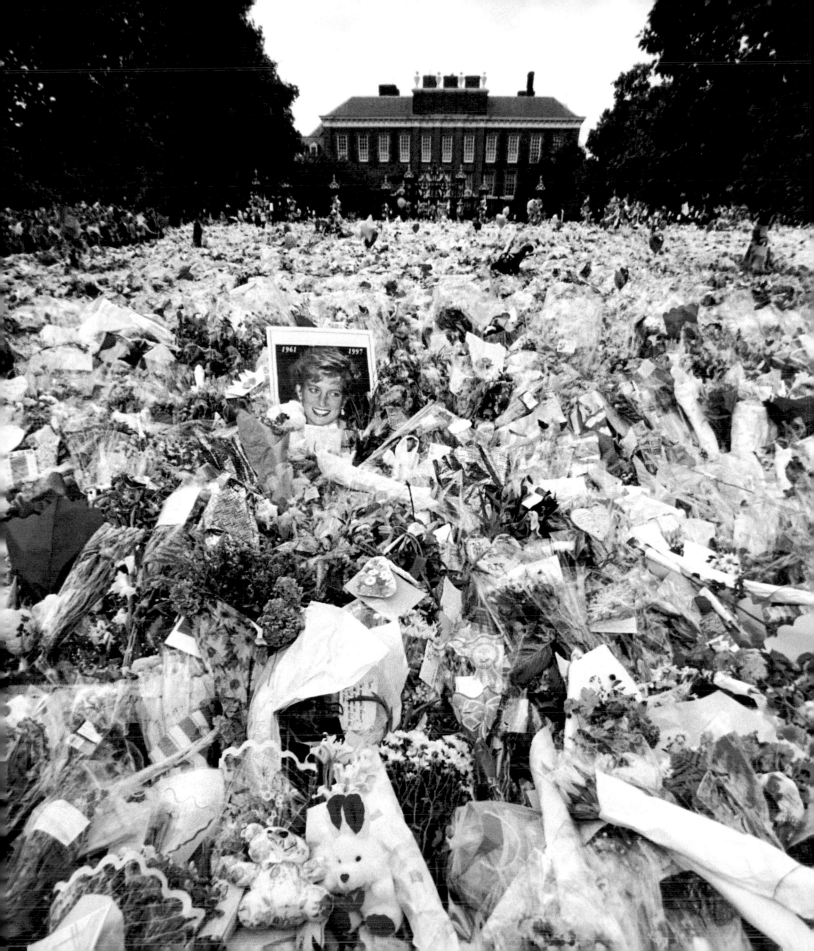

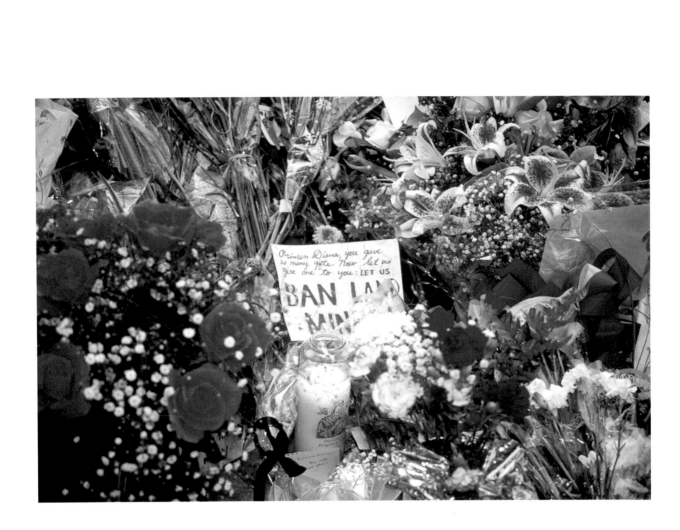

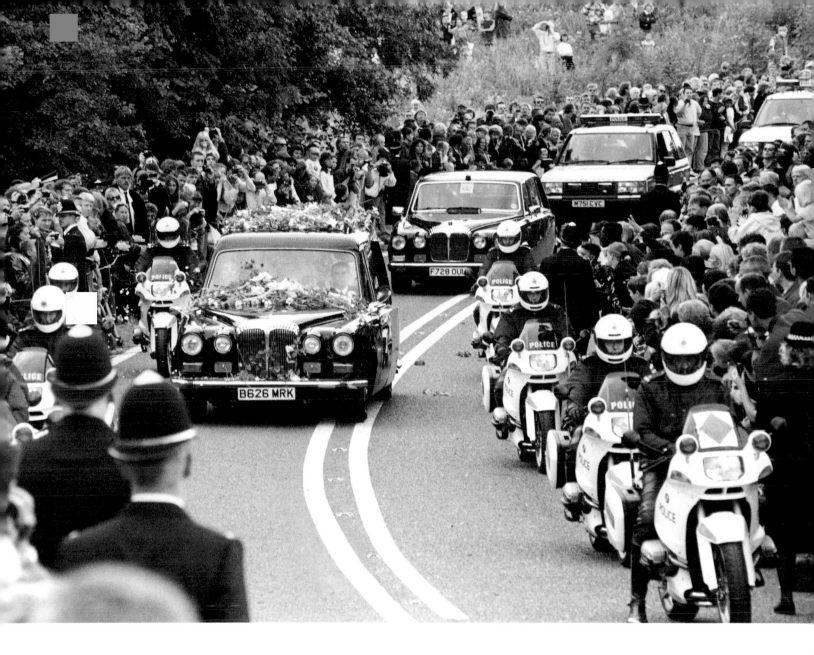

The hearse arrives at Althorp in Northamptonshire

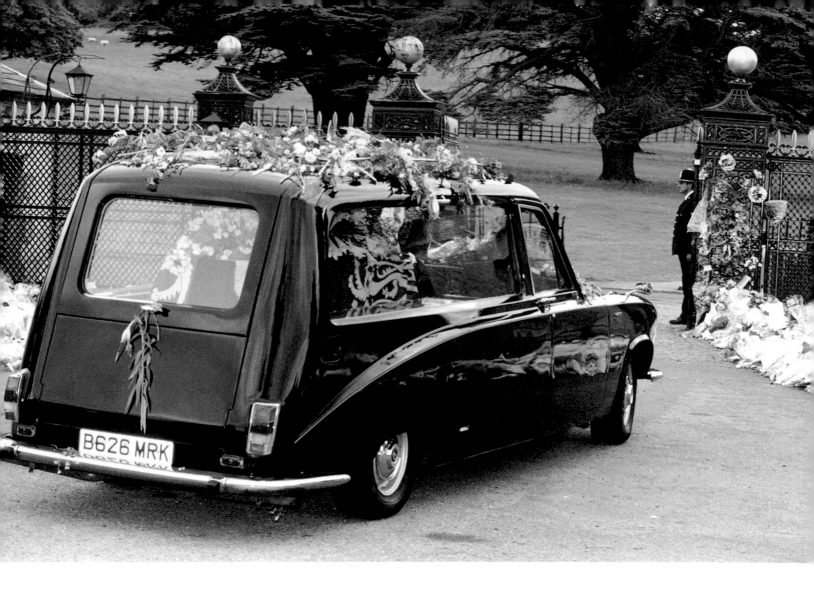

The local girl beloved of the world was returning home for the last time. As she disappeared through the gates of the estate, offering the photographers the last pictures they would ever take of her, the curtain was drawn on one of the most remarkable days in modern British history.

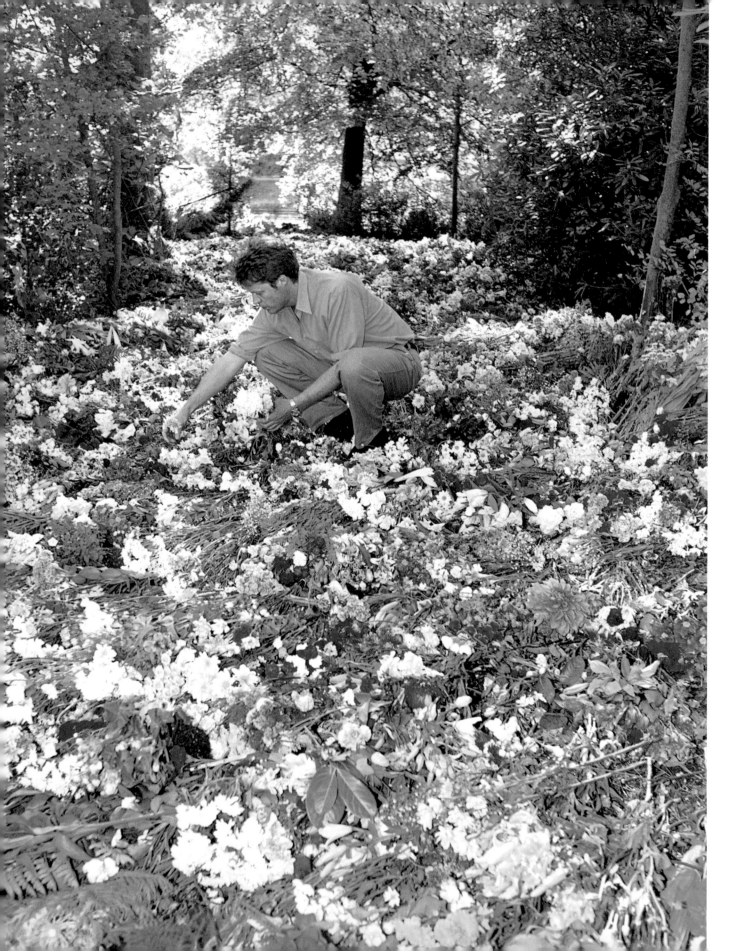

Though I speak with the tongues of men and of angels, and have not love, I am become as sounding brass, or a tinkling cymbal. And though I have the gift of prophecy, and understand all mysteries, and all knowledge; and though I have all faith, so that I could remove mountains, and have not love, I am nothing. And though I bestow all my goods to feed the poor, and though I give my body to be burned, and have not love, it profiteth me nothing.

Love suffereth long, and is kind; love envieth not; love vaunteth not itself, is not puffed up, doth not behave itself unseemly, seeketh not her own, is not easily provoked, thinketh no evil; rejoiceth not in iniquity, but rejoiceth in the truth; beareth all things, believeth all things, hopeth all things, endureth all things.

Love never faileth: but whether there be prophecies, they shall fail; whether there be tongues, they shall cease; whether there be knowledge, it shall vanish away. For we know in part, and we prophesy in part. But when that which is perfect is come, then that which is in part shall be done away.

When I was a child, I spake as a child, I understood as a child, I thought as a child: but when I became a man, I put away childish things. For now we see through a glass, darkly; but then face to face: now I know in part; but then shall I know even as also I am known. And now abideth faith, hope, love, these three; but the greatest of these is love.

1 CORINTHIANS, 13

Charles Spencer took the people's flowers from the gates of Althorp, and placed them on the island where his sister lies buried.

Overleaf, the flowers at Kensington Palace.

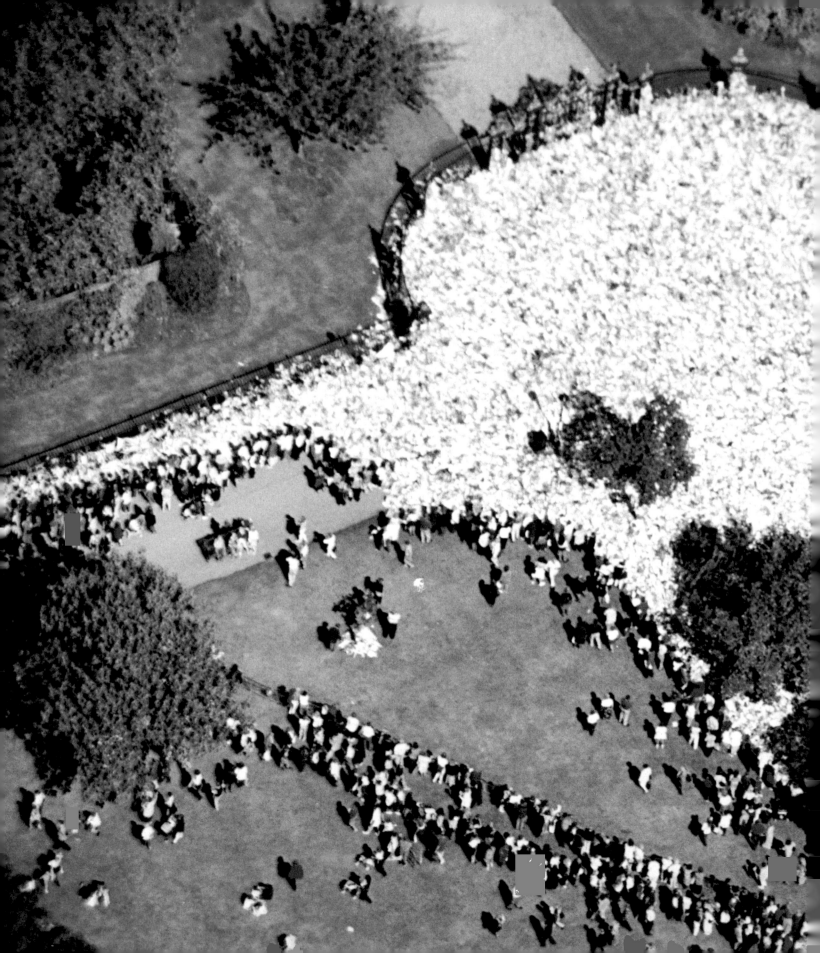

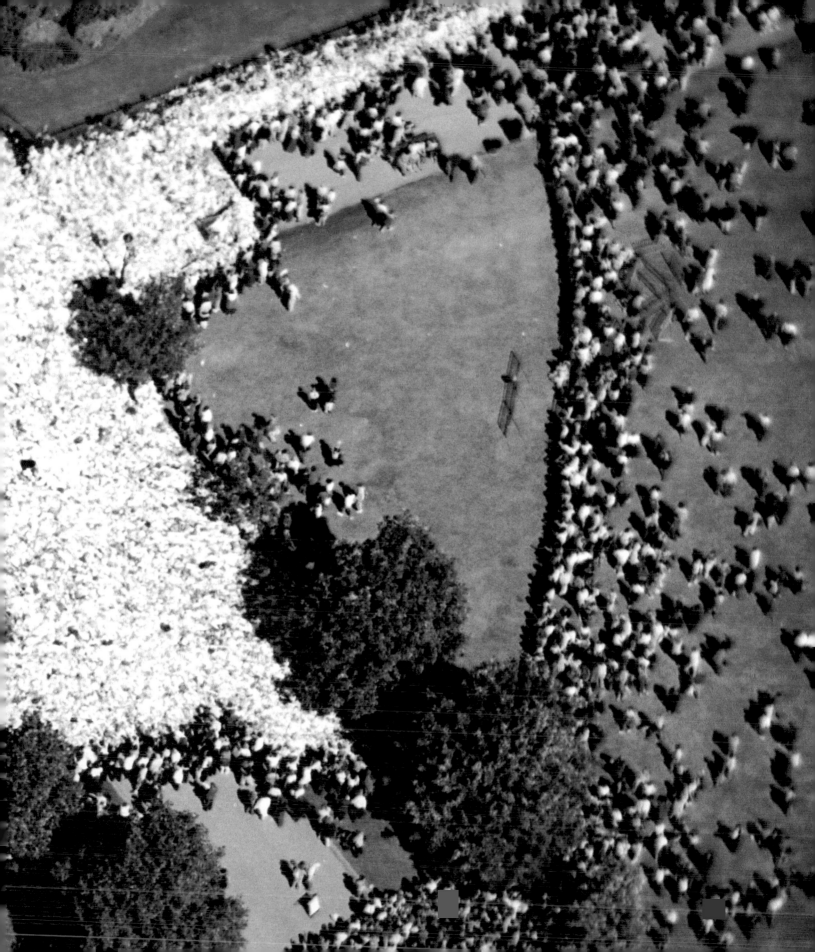

Diana's funeral was attended, via television, by some 2.5 billion people around the world, getting on for half the earth's population. In London, the route of the procession had been lengthened to accommodate the crowds, by public demand, and for fear that people might die in the crush to mourn her. Thousands slept out on the streets overnight, knowing that nothing like this would happen again in their lifetimes. There had been no comparable event in British history.

Only 2,000 mourners could be crammed into Westminster Abbey, but at least they included as many true friends, colleagues and beneficiaries of the dead Princess as the great and the good who are usually allowed to hijack these occasions. Again, "people power" had won the day, ensuring that world leaders and European monarchs were less entitled to ex-officio seats than people who had actually known Diana, cared about her, loved her. Before the day was through, they were to become part of another unexpected, quite unprecedented display of the popular will.

Women wailed, in a very un-British way, as the coffin left Kensington Palace on its four-mile journey to the Abbey. As it passed Buckingham Palace the Queen, who bows to no one, inclined her head towards her dead ex-daughter-in-law, the free spirit whose banishment from her family was now causing her such grief. As it passed St James's Palace, where it had lain all week, Diana's sons joined the procession to walk solemnly behind it, flanked by their father, uncle and grandfather. William could scarcely lift his head all the way, while young Harry braved his life's worst ordeal with remarkable composure.

After Diana's favourite passage from the Verdi *Requiem*, Elton John dragged the monarchy further towards the present day by singing a pop song – "Candle in the Wind", his elegy for Marilyn Monroe, with new words specially written for his friend Diana. As its last tender strains died away, the applause from the crowd outside could be clearly heard in the Abbey. Then Diana's brother, Charles, unleashed a tribute which turned into a tirade, against the media who had dogged his sister's life, and the royal family who had tried to reclaim her in death. Before the world, he pledged to his dead sister that her "blood family" would do all in its power to continue "the imaginative, loving way" in which she had been bringing up her sons, "so that their souls are not immersed by duty and tradition, but can sing as openly as you planned".

As Charles Spencer's voice cracked with emotion, the applause outside began again. This time, despite the implied insult to the senior royals in the midst of the congregation, it invaded the ancient Abbey, starting at the back, then creeping down the sides until the entire church apart from the Windsors was clapping. Even poor William and Harry, blinded by grief and untrained in royal protocol, joined in. It was the nearest the House of Windsor has yet come to face-to-face rejection, the moment it knew for sure that it must change to survive.

Diana was causing trouble again, even from within a stately coffin draped in the royal standard. The wailing continued afterwards, as it was placed in the hearse for the eighty-mile drive to Althorp. Crowds lined the entire route, right up the M1 motorway, throwing flowers in such profusion that the driver had to stop to clear the windscreen. By the time it reached her childhood home, its path strewn with floral tributes, the hearse's sombre black was garlanded in the bright colours of nature. The local girl beloved of the world was returning home for the last time. As she disappeared through the gates of the estate, offering the photographers the last pictures they would ever take of her, the curtain was drawn on one of the most remarkable days in modern British history. The will of the people had opened up a seismic fault beneath the 1,000-year-old British monarchy, shaken to its foundations by the popular feeling for a free-spirited force of nature, loved all the more by the people for her rejection by the royals.

She was buried on an island in a lake at the heart of the estate, which she had loved in childhood, and where her sons can now visit her in privacy whenever they want, while the rest of the world gains occasional access to pay its lasting homage. Within hours that island too was carpeted with flowers, hiding the scars in the earth which had finally quenched Diana's abundant spirit.

The royal family retreated to Balmoral that same evening, but it was to take days yet for Britain to return to anything remotely approaching normal. The signal, again by popular will, came four evenings later at Wembley, the national soccer stadium, when a vital World Cup qualifying match was preceded by a minute's silence for Diana. The 75,000 crowd wept again, cradling their candles against the wind, as Elton John's elegy echoed around the country one more time. But Elton himself had said that day that it was now "time for life to go on". And the referee's whistle, by universal consent, signified the freedom to stop talking about Diana in hushed tones, and honour her memory with smiles, cheers and laughter. The England players, all wearing black arm bands, dedicated their performance that night to her memory. They won 4-0.

As darkness fell eighty miles away, ten days after her death had convulsed the nation she loved, just who lay buried on that island? As it falls again tonight, who lies there now? A beautiful young mother, cruelly cut off in her prime? An incarnate idea whose time had come, inspiring Britain to cast off its post-imperial shackles and look to its European future? A martyr to the media age? Or a saint in the making, who by her own example has turned us all into better people?

MEMORIES

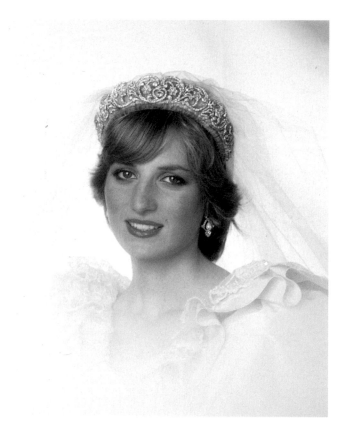

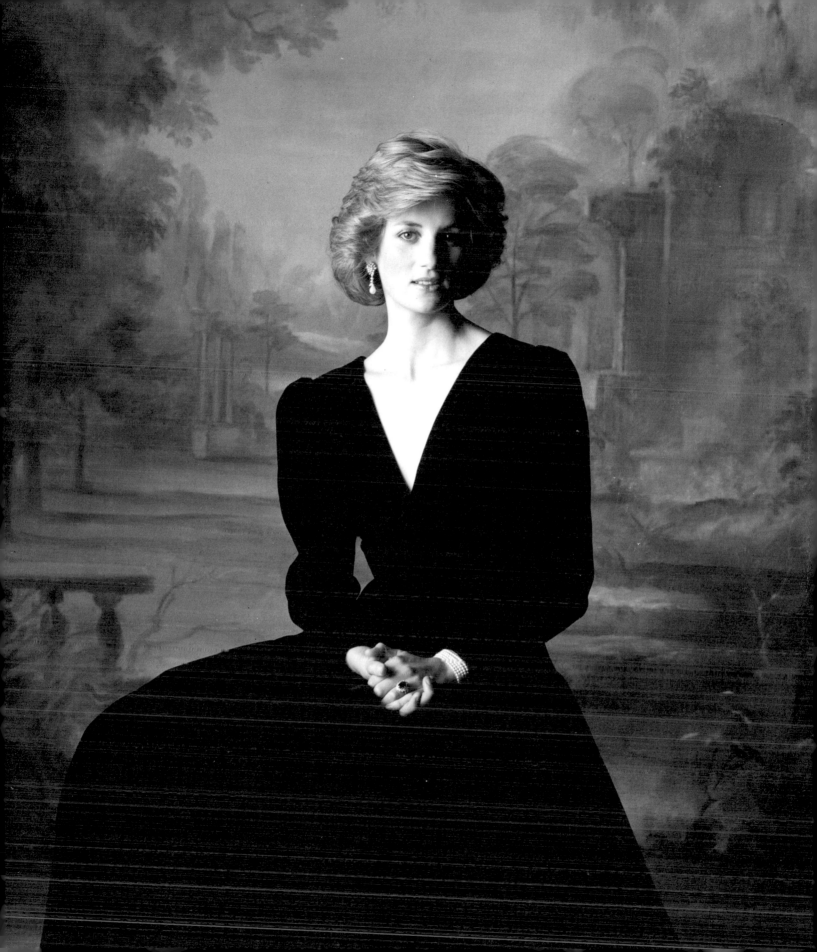

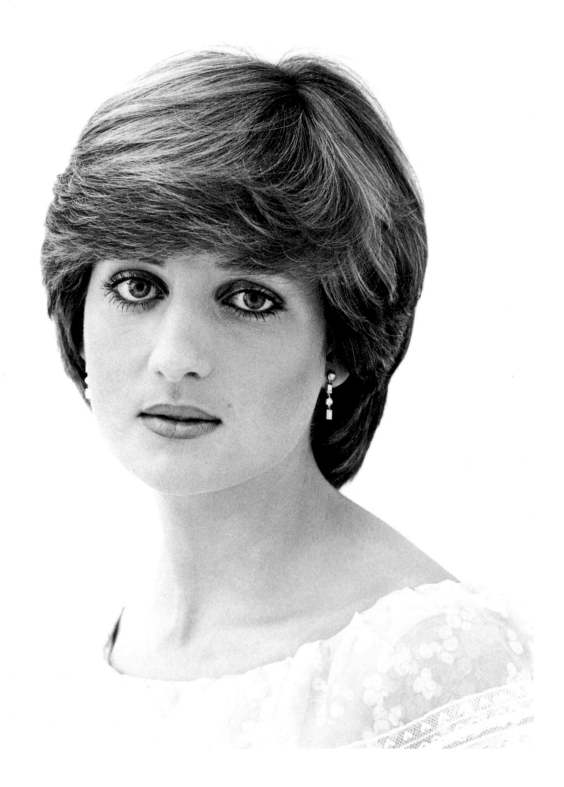

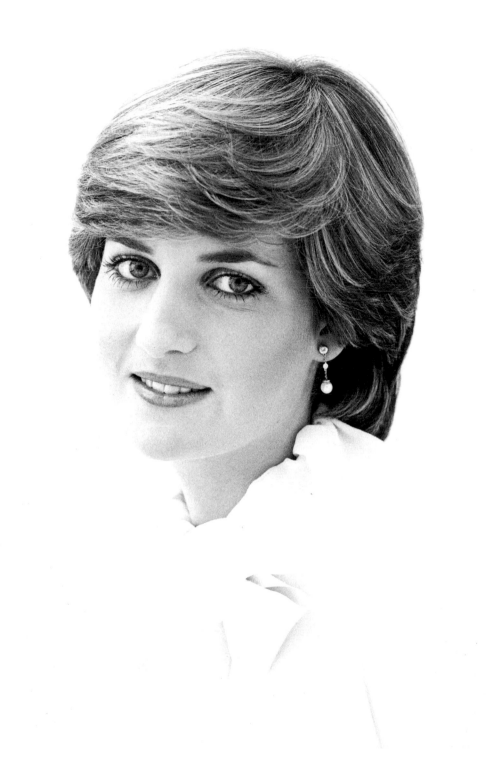

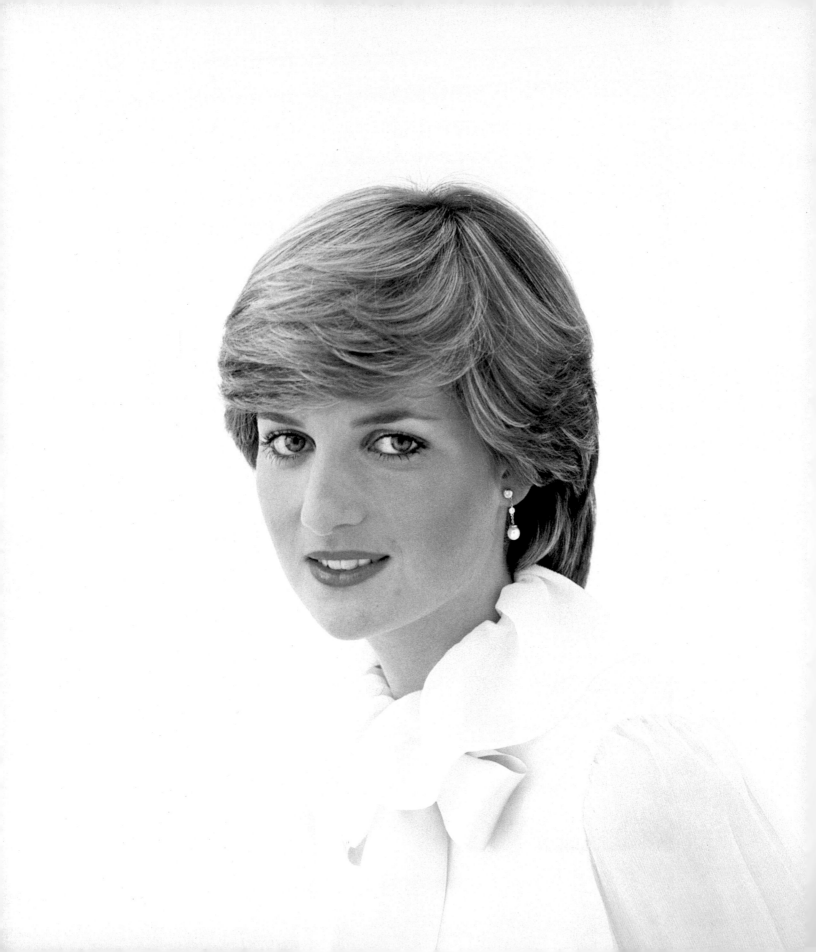

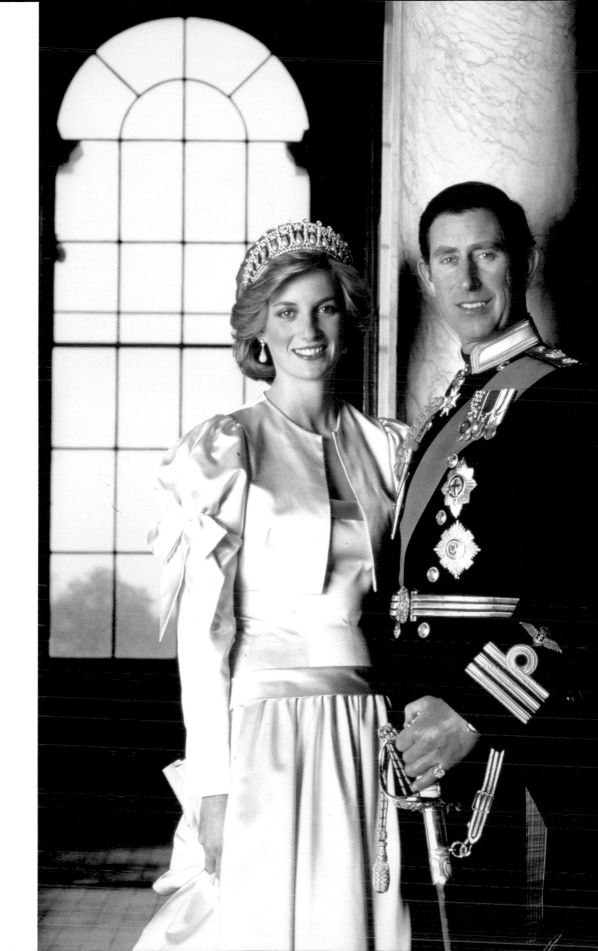

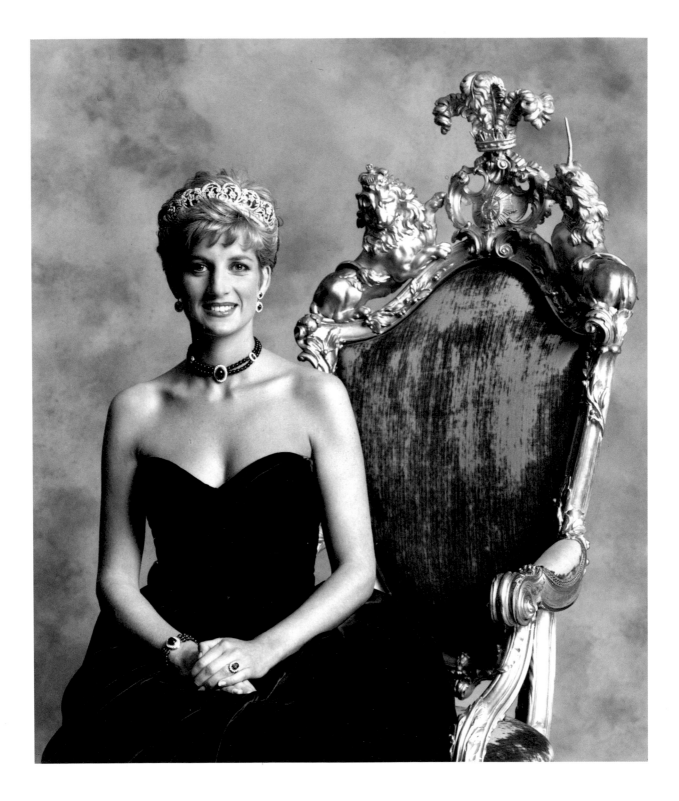

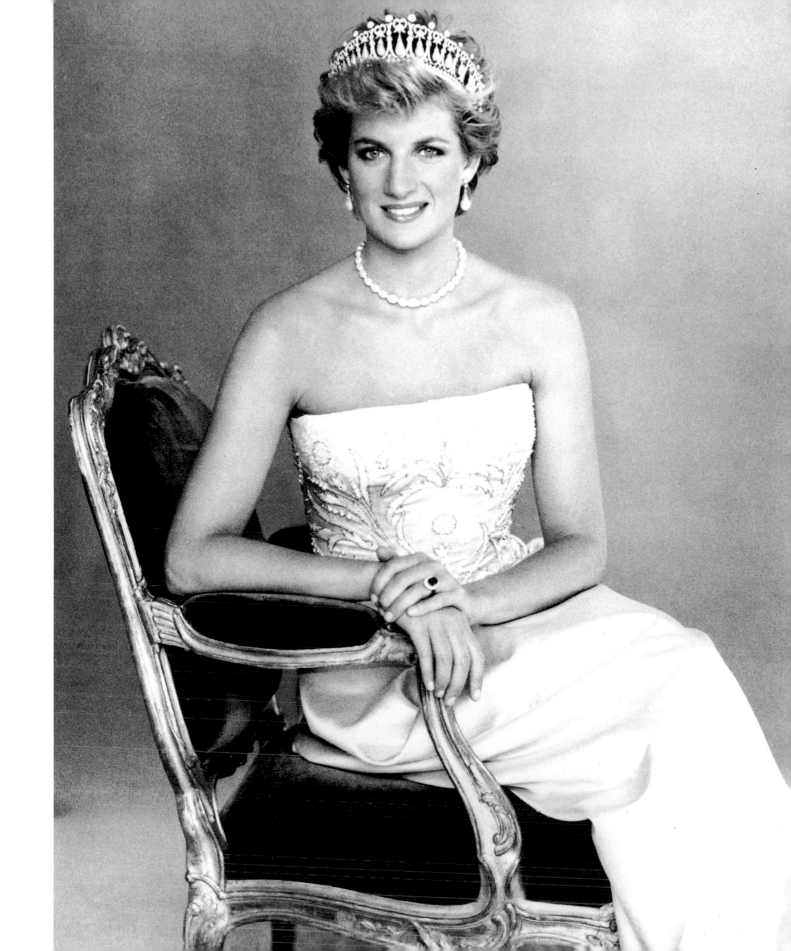

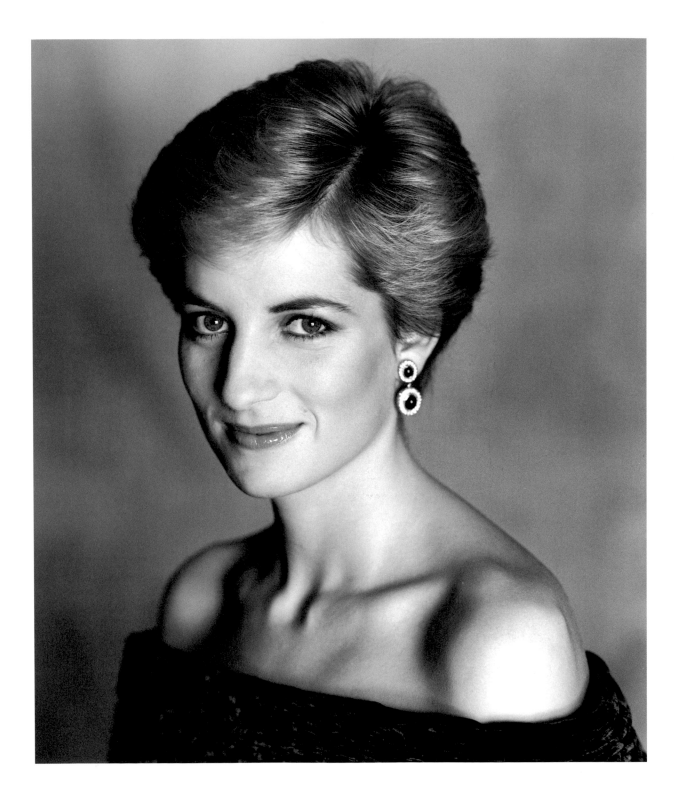

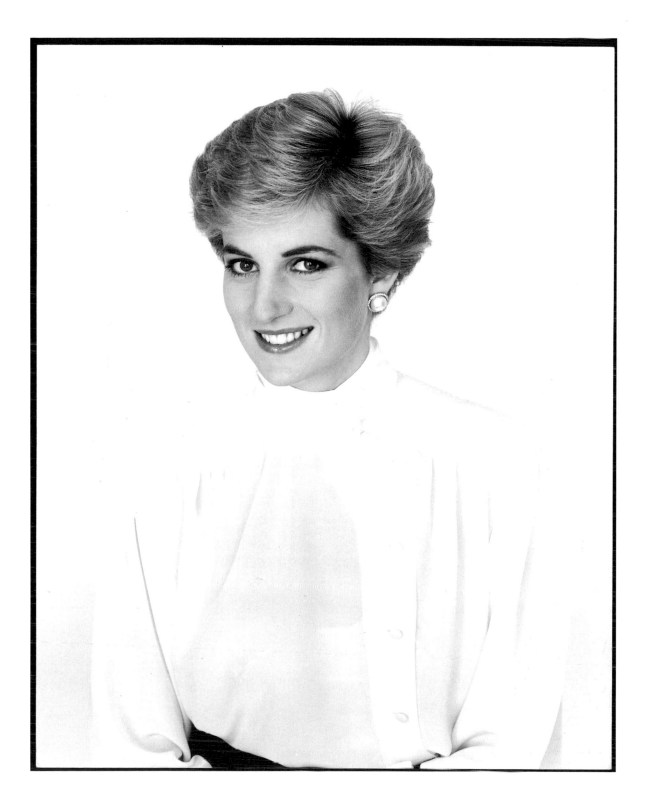

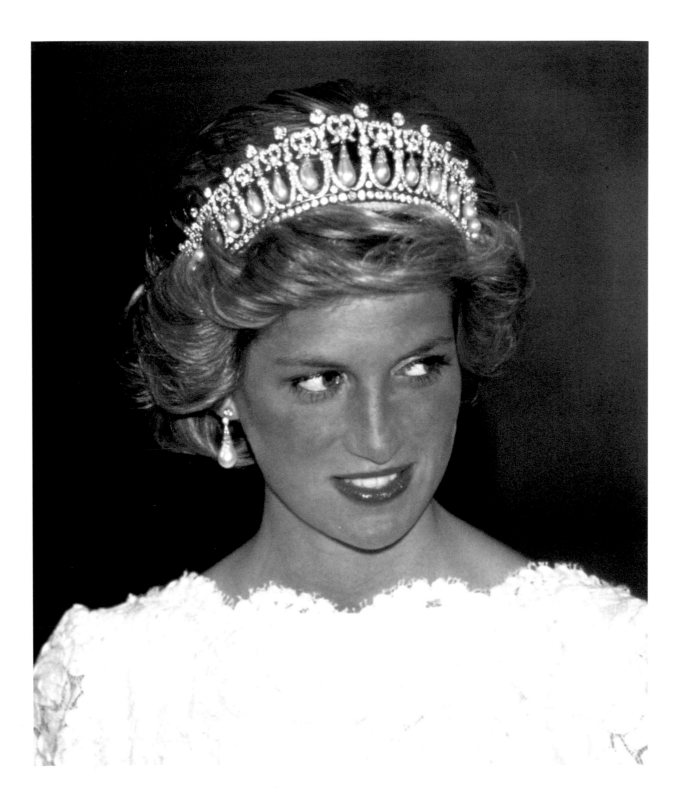

"A very insecure person at heart, almost childlike in her desire to do good for others so she could release herself from deep feelings of unworthiness.... The world sensed this part of her character, and cherished her for her vulnerability while admiring her for her honesty."

— THE EARL SPENCER

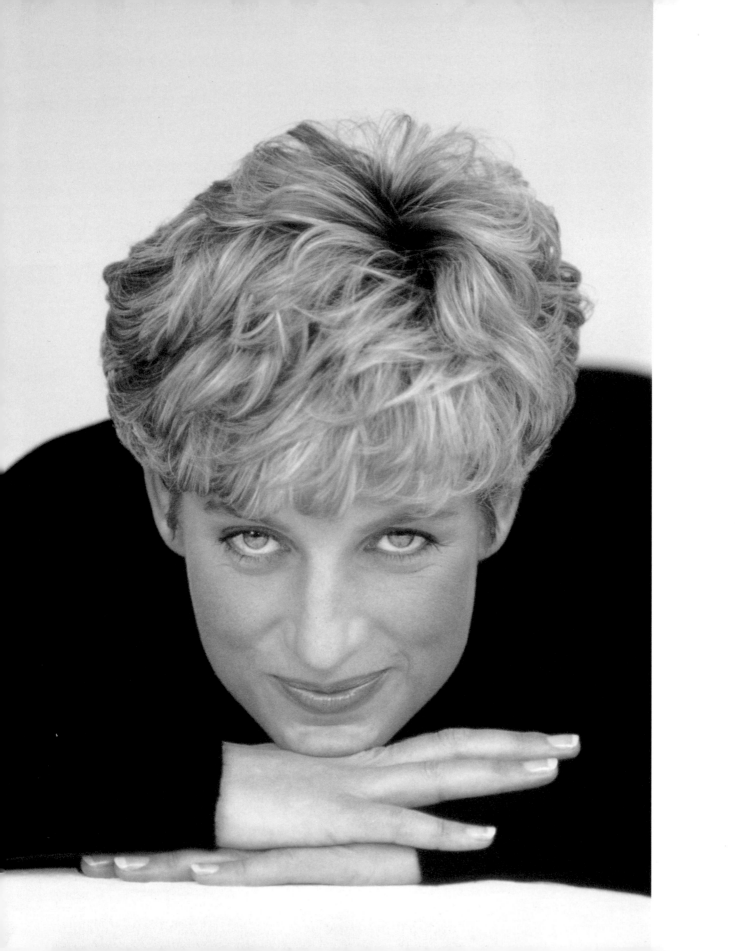

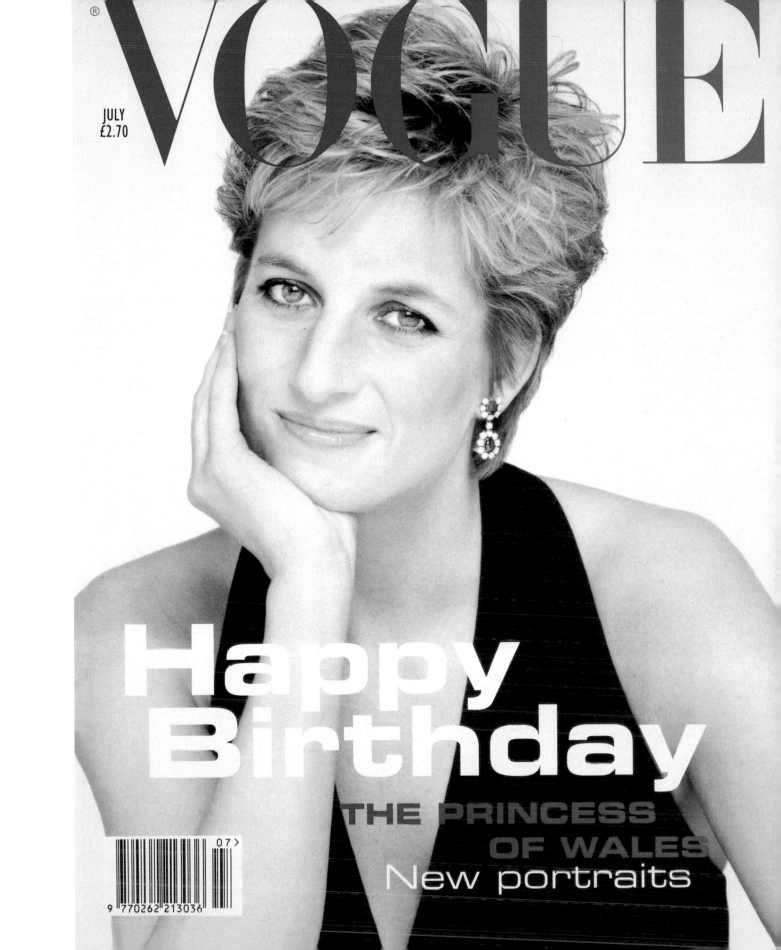

VOGUE

JULY
£2.70

Happy Birthday
THE PRINCESS OF WALES
New portraits

07>

9 770262 213036

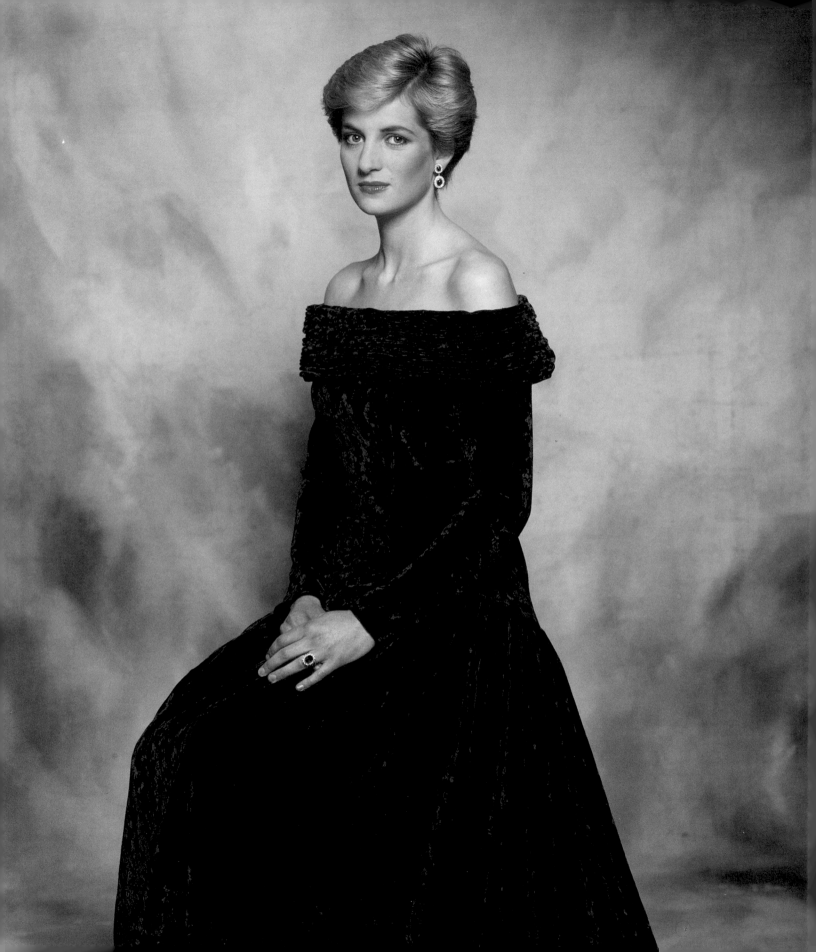

Behind the stylish and glamorous facade lay continuing doubts and uncertainties, a fundamental lack of self-esteem, even self-belief, which was to haunt her all her life.

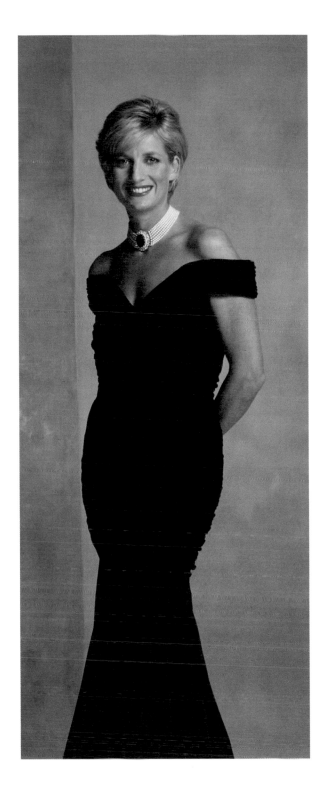

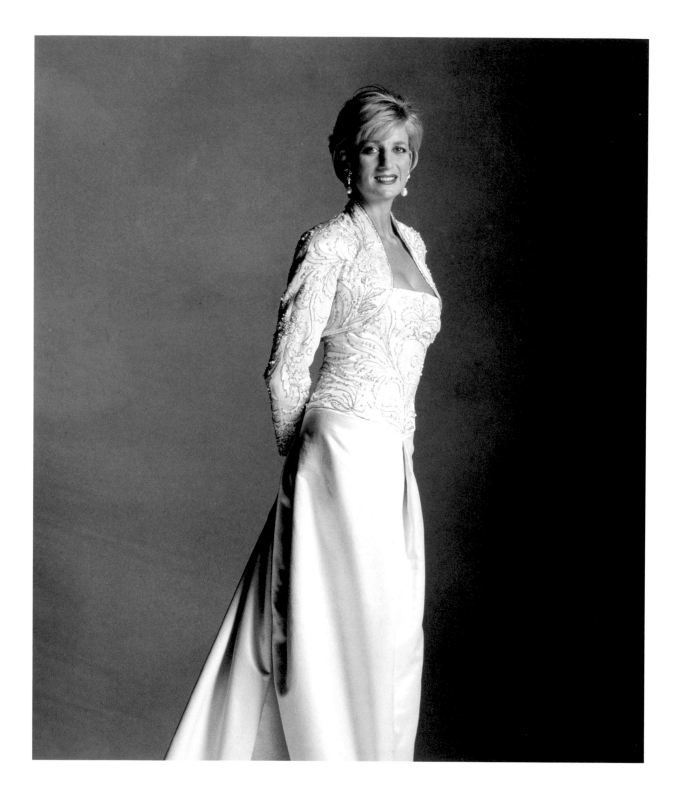

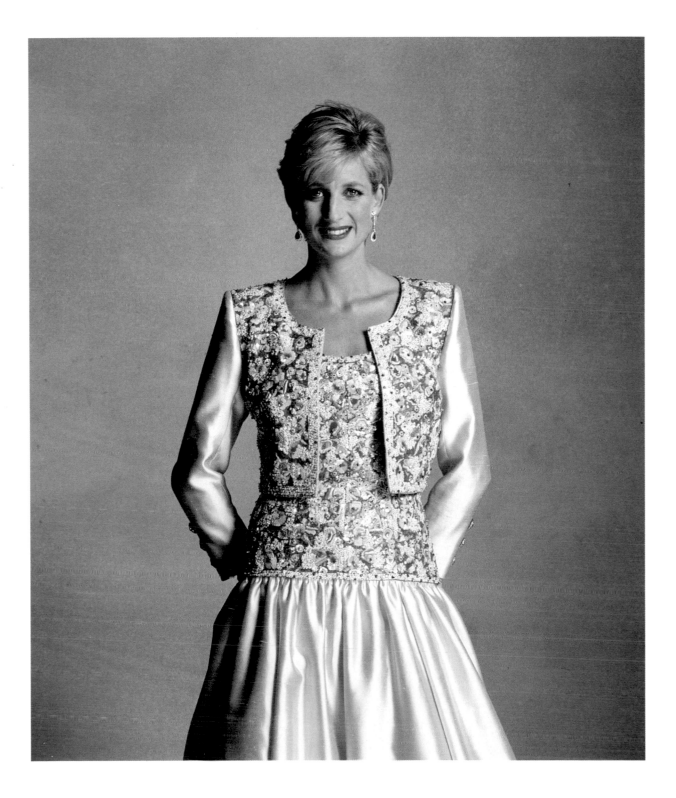

By the end of her life, it was not just that Diana at last seemed to have found a little happiness. She was beginning to show the self-confidence she had always lacked. The abandoned child, "shy Di", the gleaming fashion plate, the caring mother, the rejected wife, the royal outcast – all were eventually to merge in a uniquely contemporary figure with many complex layers of apparently boundless appeal. Once this particular Cinderella had stamped her glass slipper, with a crash that echoed around the world, she became an icon to the one group who had so far spurned her, the feminist movement, who now adopted her as a role model to speak for all womankind. Even then, however, there were strains of the Diana myth which ran distinctly deeper.

We must remember her as the gentle, caring, confused, at times infuriating human being – a real "handful", to her devoted friend Clive James – so movingly recalled by those who really knew her. "A very insecure person at heart," to her brother Charles, "almost childlike in her desire to do good for others so she could release herself from feelings of unworthiness." To Rosa Monckton, she was "complicated on the one hand, and simple and naive on the other. These two co-existed, sometimes awkwardly, and made her life more difficult than it should have been. Her dark side was that of a wounded, trapped animal, and her bright side was that of a luminous being." Both this luminous being and the trapped animal are important to hold on to, for they are in danger of vanishing into the myth. In death, as was perhaps inevitable, the very human being that was Diana swiftly began to get lost amid the archetypes. Now, gradually, they will take over, and they are unlikely to let her rest in peace.

Their foremost archivist is the American writer Camille Paglia, to whom the scope of Diana's appeal was far more than a case study in the modern cult of celebrity, more than merely high-class soap opera or "a reactionary wish-fulfilment fantasy for American Anglophiles". To Paglia, Diana tapped into "certain deep and powerful strains" akin to "atavistic religious emotions". The unfolding story of her life had turned into a potent procession of archetypes.

From Cinderella she metamorphosed via the Betrayed Wife ("tricked and manoeuvred into impregnation by Satan"), into Rapunzel, the Princess imprisoned in the Tower, surrounded by scheming courtiers, awaiting rescue by a gallant knight on a white charger. At this stage of her baroque story, Diana was a symbol redolent of pre-Raphaelite images by Holman Hunt or Millais, Tennyson's Lady of Shalott or Keats's half-mad young widow Isabella, even Burne-Jones's Andromeda Chained to the Rock.

Next came the *Mater Dolorosa*, a neo-Renaissance Madonna, "a modern Mary with a taste for rock 'n' roll". This ran parallel with the Pagan Goddess, a Graeco-Roman image of Diana as the huntress, "a fierce Italian goddess of the woods, ranged against her enemy Camilla, Virgil's Amazon, the militant Volscian horsewoman". Off duty, of course, a sultry temptress by the Caribbean Sea, she was Botticelli's Venus, with a "persistent, half-conscious provocativeness" – also reflected in the clothes she sometimes chose for public appearances, showing the world rather more of herself than is royalty's way. But deification, as Paglia wrote in 1992, has its price. "The modern mega-celebrity, bearing the burden of collective symbolism, projection and fantasy, is a ritual victim, cannibalised by our pity and fear.... Those at the apex of the social pyramid are untouchables, condemned to horrifying solitude.... Diana the huntress is now the hind paralysed in the world's gun sight." How uncannily Earl Spencer would echo these words five years later, at the funeral of the woman the world now knew as that victim: "A girl given the name of the ancient goddess of hunting was, in the end, the most hunted person of the modern age."

Diana, Princess of Wales has a thousand such epitaphs, some offered by names almost as resonant as hers, from Mother Teresa to Nelson Mandela, many more by names the world has never heard of, and never will – people Diana had never met, and now never would. But the most fitting, to my mind, is one short, simple sentence of her own, which came as always from the heart, and speaks with the plain, unvarnished directness which was ever the hallmark of the human being – as frail and flawed as the rest of us – behind the myth.

 "When I go home and turn off my light at night," she once said, "I know that I did my best."

Now that her own light has been extinguished, so cruelly and prematurely, we who survive and mourn Diana, we whose lives she so enriched, must in turn do our best for her.

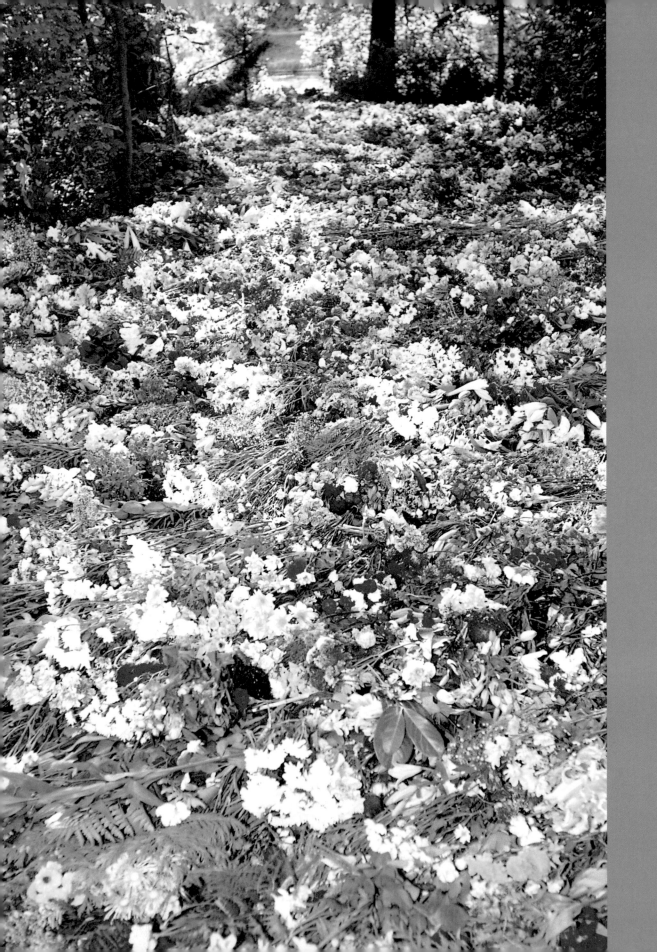

"I am a free spirit."

ACKNOWLEDGEMENTS

Page 1 Giza, Egypt, 1992: Nils Jorgensen, Rex Features. 5 Leaving the Ritz Hotel: Alan Davidson, Camera Press. 7 1990: Patrick Demarchelier, Camera Press. 8 Harefield Hospital, Middlesex, 1996: Rex Features. 10 *Panorama* interview, 1995: Rex Features. 11 Northwick Park Hospital, 1997: Rex Features. 12 Australia, 1983: Rex Features. 14 Gemma Levine, Camera Press. 16 At Highgrove, 1990: Patrick Demarchelier, British *Vogue*/Camera Press. 17 Sarajevo, 1997: Popperfoto/Reuter. 18 With Mother Teresa, New York, 1997: Mike Segar, Popperfoto/Reuter. 20 Park House, Sandringham, aged 2: Press Association/RBO/Camera Press. 21 Park House, aged 3: Press Association/RBO/Camera Press. 22 Park House, early 1960s: Press Association/RBO/Camera Press. 23 Cadogan Place Gardens, London, 1968: Press Association/RBO/Camera Press. 24 With Charles, Viscount Althorp, at Park House, 1967: Press Association/RBO/Camera Press. 25 Berkshire, 1968: Press Association/RBO/Camera Press. 26 Croquet at Itchenor, West Sussex, 1970: Press Association/RBO/Camera Press. 27 Itchenor, West Sussex, 1970: Press Association/RBO/Camera Press. 28-9 Oban, Scotland, 1974: Press Association/RBO/Camera Press. 33 Rex Features. 34 1980: Charles de la Court, Camera Press. 35 1981: Snowdon, Camera Press. 36 Backstage at Buckingham Palace, 1981: Patrick Lichfield, Camera Press. 37 The royal wedding, 1981: Camera Press. 38 1981: Patrick Lichfield, Camera Press. 39 Patrick Lichfield, Camera Press. 40 Balmoral, 1981: Mauro Carraro, Rex Features. 41 Mauro Carraro, Rex Features. 42 Balmoral, 1981: Bill Cooper, Rex Features. 43 Newcastle, 1983: Lionel Cherruault, Camera Press. 44 Gibraltar, 1981: Bryn Colton, Camera Press. 45T Polo, 1987: Brendan Beirne, Rex Features. 45BL Polo, 1987: Brendan Beirne, Rex Features. 45BR 1992: Arthur Edwards, Popperfoto/Reuter. 46 Ayer's Rock, Australia, 1983: Rex Features. 47 Hyde Park, London, 1994: Popperfoto/Reuter. 49 Popperfoto. 50 With Princess Grace of Monaco, Goldsmith's Hall, London, 1981: Rex Features. 51 With the Duchess of York, Ascot, 1992: Ken Goff, Camera Press. 53T David Hartley, Rex Features. 53BL J. Sutton Hibbert, Rex Features. 53BR JS Library. 55 *Panorama* interview, 1995: Rex Features. 56 Birth of Prince William, 1982: Jon Bennett, Camera Press. 57 Prince William, 1982: Snowdon, Camera Press. 58 Royal tour of New Zealand: JS Library. 59 Christening of Prince Harry, 1984: Snowdon, Camera Press. 60 Snowdon, Camera Press. 61 Snowdon, Camera Press. 62 Glenn Harvey, Camera Press. 63 Glenn Harvey, Camera Press. 64 John Shelley, Rex Features. 65 Rex Features. 66 Julian Herbert, Camera Press. 67 David Hartley, Rex Features. 68L Glenn Harvey, Camera Press. 68R Anwar Hussein, All Action. 69L Brendan Beirne, Rex Features. 69R Popperfoto. 70 Patrick Demarchelier, British *Vogue*/Camera Press. 71 Patrick Demarchelier, British *Vogue*/Camera Press. 72 Patrick Demarchelier, British *Vogue*/Camera Press. 73 Patrick Demarchelier, British *Vogue*/Camera Press. 74L Rex Features. 74R Popperfoto. 75 Glenn Harvey, Camera Press. 76 Today/Rex Features. 77T Bob Collier, *Sunday Times*/Camera Press. 77B Rex Features. 78-9 National Deaf-Blind and Rubella Association, Ealing, West London, 1984: Roy Letkey, Popperfoto/Reuter. 80 Anwar Hussein, All Action. 81 Popperfoto/Reuter. 82 Jim Bennett, Camera Press. 83 Rex Features. 84 *Sun*/Rex Features. 85 Vladimir Sichov, Sipa Press/Rex Features. 86 Rota/Camera Press. 87 Thompson/Popperfoto. 88-9 Glenn Harvey, Camera Press. 91 Rex Features. 93 Tim Rooke, Rex Features. 97 Bryn Colton, Rex Features. 98 Rex Features. 99 Rex Features. 100 Glenn Harvey, Camera Press. 101 Martin Godwin, Camera Press. 102-3 JS Library. 105T Dave Hartley, Rex Features. 105BL Rex Features. 105BR Rex Features. 106 Rex Features. 107 Rex Features. 108L Mauro Carrea, Rex Features. 108R L. Cherruault, Camera Press. 109 Rex Features. 110L Anwar Hussein. 110M JS Library. 110R Anwar Hussein. 111 Brendan Beirne, Rex Features. 112 JS Library. 113 Popperfoto/Reuter. 115 Rex Features. 116 Peter Nicholls, Rex Features. 117 Peter Nicholls, Rex Features. 118 Anwar Hussein. 119 A. Edwards, Camera Press. 120 Anwar Hussein. 121 Anwar Hussein. 122-3 Prince Charles with Lady Diana Spencer, Goldsmith's Hall, 1981: LNS/Camera Press. 124-5 Rex Features. 126 Anwar Hussein. 127 Anwar Hussein. 128 Mother Teresa, New York, 1997: Mike Segar, Popperfoto/Reuter. 129 Charles Sykes, Rex Features. 130 Concert to mark 10th anniversary of the Prince's Trust, June 1986: David Osborn, Popperfoto/Reuter. 131 Mauro Carraro, Rex Features. 132 Demarthon/AFP/Popperfoto. 133 Rota, Camera Press. 134 Rex Features. 135 Juda Ngwenya, Popperfoto/Reuter. 136 International Red Cross, Luanda, Angola, 1997: Tim Rooke/Rex Features. 137 Glenn Harvey, Camera Press. 138 Tim Rooke, Rex Features. 139 Tim Rooke, Rex Features. 140 With the Angolan Foreign Minister in Luanda: Juda Ngwenya, Popperfoto/Reuter. 141 Rex Features. 142 Tim Rooke, Rex Features. 143 Tim Rooke, Rex Features. 144-5 Tim Rooke, Rex Features. 147 Theodore Wood, Camera Press. 148 Fiona Hanson, Press Association. 149 John Giles, Press Association. 150 Adam Butler, Press Association. 152 John Stillwell, Press Association. 154 Paul Barker, Press Association. 155 Rebecca Naden, Press Association. 156 Dave Cheskin, Press Association. 157 Simon Schluter, Rex Features. 158 Barry Batchelor, Press Association. 159 J. Sutton Hibbert, Rex Features. 160 Peter Heismath, Rex Features. 161 David Jones, Press Association. 162 David Jones, Press Association. 164 David Jones, Press Association. 166-7 Adrian Dennis, Rex Features. 170 Patrick Lichfield, Camera Press. 171 Snowdon, Camera Press. 172 Snowdon, British *Vogue*/Camera Press. 173 Snowdon, British *Vogue*/Camera Press. 174 Snowdon, Camera Press. 175 Snowdon, Camera Press. 176 Snowdon, Camera Press. 177 Patrick Demarchelier, Camera Press. 178 Terence Donovan, Camera Press. 179 Terence Donovan, Camera Press. 180 Glenn Harvey, Camera Press. 182 Patrick Demarchelier, Camera Press. 183 1994 Patrick Demarchelier, © British *Vogue*/The Condé Nast Publications Ltd. 184 Terence Donovan, Camera Press. 185 Snowdon, Camera Press. 186 Snowdon, Camera Press. 187 Snowdon, Camera Press. 190 David Jones, Press Association.

The poem "If I should die" on page 151 is by A. Price Hughes. The second reading is entitled "Time". Its author is unknown.